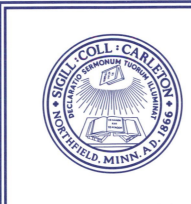

## A CONCISE HANDBOOK OF MOVIE INDUSTRY ECONOMICS

This concise handbook collects essays on all aspects of the motion picture industry by leading authorities in political economy, economics, accounting, finance, and marketing. In addition to bringing the reader an up-to-date perspective on what is known and what has been accomplished, it includes both new findings on a variety of topics and directions for additional research. Topics include the estimation of theatrical and ancillary demand, profitability studies, resolution of evident paradoxes in studio executive behavior, interaction of the industry and government, impacts of the most recent changes in accounting standards, and the role and importance of participation contracts. New results include findings on the true nature of the seasonality of theatrical demand, the predictive power of surveys based on trailers, the impact of the Academy Awards, the effectiveness of prior history measures to gauge cast members and directors, and the substitutability of movies across different genres.

Charles C. Moul is Assistant Professor of Economics at Washington University in St. Louis. His work documenting evidence of how movie quality improved as studios gained experience with synchronous-sound recording (i.e., "talkie") technology has appeared in the *Journal of Industrial Economics*. Professor Moul's ongoing research addresses whether economics is a valid and useful tool to analyze as volatile a process as weekly movie demand, how demand for a movie saturates as the pool of potential consumers views it, and the value of advertising to society. In April 2003, he organized and hosted *Entertainment Economics: The Movie Industry*, a conference bringing together leading authorities in digital production, copyright law, marketing, economics, accounting, and regulation.

# A Concise Handbook of

# Movie Industry Economics

Edited by

**CHARLES C. MOUL**
Washington University in St. Louis

CAMBRIDGE UNIVERSITY PRESS
Cambridge, New York, Melbourne, Madrid, Cape Town, Singapore, São Paulo

Cambridge University Press
40 West 20th Street, New York, NY 10011-4211, USA

www.cambridge.org
Information on this title: www.cambridge.org/9780521843843

© Cambridge University Press 2005

First published 2005

Printed in the United States of America

*A catalog record for this book is available from the British Library.*

*Library of Congress Cataloging in Publication Data*

A concise handbook of movie industry economics / edited by Charles C. Moul.
p.   cm.
Includes bibliographical references and index.
ISBN 0-521-84384-7
1. Motion picture industry – Economic aspects – United States.   I. Moul, Charles C., 1972–
PN1993.5.U6S493   2005
384′.83′0973 – dc22       2004051993

ISBN-13   978-0-521-84384-3 hardback
ISBN-10   0-521-84384-7 hardback

# Contents

# Contents

# Contributors

**Jehoshua Eliashberg** is Sebastian S. Kresge Professor of Marketing and Professor of Operations and Information Management at the Wharton School of Business. In addition to holding editorial positions in leading marketing journals, his research has appeared in the *Journal of Marketing*, *Journal of Economic Psychology, Marketing Science, Journal of Marketing Research*, and *Management Science*. He is the inaugural winner of the Mallen prize for published scholarly contributions to motion-picture–industry studies.

**Charles C. Moul** is Assistant Professor of Economics at Washington University in St. Louis. He received his doctorate in economics from Northwestern University in 2000 upon completion of his dissertation, "Empirical Essays on the Motion Picture Industry." His work on movies has appeared in the *Journal of Industrial Economics*, and his current work on theatrical distribution emphasizes implications of demand saturation and the impacts of advertising.

**S. Abraham Ravid** is Professor of Finance at Rutgers University. He has contributed articles to leading finance and economics journals including the *Journal of Finance, Journal of Business, Journal of Financial and*

*Quantitative Analysis, Quarterly Journal of Economics,* and *Bell Journal of Economics.* Prior to receiving his Ph.D., he was a professional journalist.

**Steven M. Shugan** is Professor of Marketing at the University of Florida, where he holds the Russell Berrie Eminent Scholar Chair. His work has been published in leading marketing journals including *Marketing Science, Journal of Marketing,* and *Management Science.* In addition to consulting for more than twenty different firms, he has served on a number of editorial boards. He is currently Editor-in-Chief of *Marketing Science.*

**Harold L. Vogel** is the author of *Entertainment Industry Economics: A Guide for Financial Analysis* (Sixth Edition, 2004) and of the companion volume, *Travel Industry Economics: A Guide for Financial Analysis* (2001), both published by Cambridge University Press. He was ranked as top entertainment industry analyst for a record ten years by *Institutional Investor* magazine and was the senior entertainment industry analyst at Merrill Lynch for seventeen years.

**Janet Wasko** is Professor of Communication at the University of Oregon, Eugene. The political economy of communications, its structure and policies, is the focal point of her research. She is author, coauthor, or editor of ten books, most recently *Dazzled by Disney? The Global Disney Audiences Project* (2001) and *How Hollywood Works* (2003).

**Charles B. Weinberg** is the SMEV Presidents Professor and Chair of Marketing at the University of British Columbia. His work on competition and dynamics of the entertainment and communications sector has appeared in the *Journal of Marketing Research, Marketing Science, Marketing Letters,* and *Journal of Marketing.* He won the Mallen prize for published scholarly contributions to motion-picture–industry studies in 2000.

# Introduction

In 1891, Thomas Edison and W. K. Laurie Dickson invented the Kineto-scope, the earliest ancestor of the modern motion picture. Competitive pressures soon induced Edison to alter the technology to project movies rather than show them to individual viewers, and the Edison Company introduced the Projectoscope in 1896. Repeated lawsuits against competitors over alleged patent infringements proved insufficient for Edison's ambitions; in 1908, the Edison Company joined with Biograph to form the Motion Picture Patents Company. This arrangement of interlocking agreements among studios, exhibitors, and Eastman Kodak (the primary supplier of film), however, only delayed the Edison Company's fate. Antitrust rulings against the Motion Picture Patents Company and superior movies out of California eventually forced the Edison Company to sell out in 1918.

Innovation, competition, and collusion...economics has *always* been the irreplaceable tool to study the motion picture industry.

In April 2003, the Weidenbaum Center on the Economy, Government, and Public Policy, in collaboration with the Department of Economics and the Department of Film and Media Studies (all of Washington University in St. Louis), presented *Entertainment Economics: The Movie*

1

# Introduction

*Industry.* The first day of this conference was a public symposium with panels on digital technology, financing, and movie making. The second day was a scholars' conference with each of the following authors presenting research on his or her topic of expertise. This volume is the tangible product of that effort.

The six chapters that follow attempt to capture both the sequential nature of the industry and several of the different viewpoints of industry analysts. The fundamentals of the motion picture industry can be highly idiosyncratic, and the industry has consequently evolved in somewhat peculiar ways. Thus, each contributing author describes and explains particular aspects of the industry's institutional structure. The second task of each author is surveying the body of ongoing research. Several of the chapters include original findings. Each chapter concludes with potential areas of new research.

As one would expect, the various topics lend themselves to different approaches. Furthermore, each author's training and discipline amplify the uniqueness of each chapter. Political economy emphasizes institutions and a holistic perspective, economics assumes that the reality that we observe is an equilibrium of rational participants, and marketing strives to help business professionals improve their performances. What unifies these authors is the common belief that careful analysis of the motion picture industry is a worthwhile endeavor.

Janet Wasko begins the volume with "Critiquing Hollywood: The Political Economy of Motion Pictures." This overview considers approaches that are included within media or cinema studies but are not typically considered part of the neoclassical economic literature. But why has the political economy approach been applied less frequently to the movie industry than to other communications research? And to what extent do production decisions at the major studios reflect an oligopoly rather than competition?

The economic analysis of production continues with "Film Production in the Digital Age – What Do We Know about the Past and the

Future?" by S. Abraham Ravid. He focuses his attention on two topics: competing explanations of movie profitability and the role of contracts for the talent. Even in the most artistic sector of the industry, a number of issues can be illuminated by economic analysis. Do movie stars increase movie profits, or do the stars successfully capture their contributions in higher pay? Does Hollywood make too many R-rated movies? And how do differing compensation structures influence which movies are produced and which actors star in them?

Harold L. Vogel explores the truths and fallacies of film account- ing in "Movie Industry Accounting." By clearly explaining the areas of bookkeeping that are common to the movie industry and other more standard businesses, he is able to pinpoint why the industry has received its (perhaps unfair) reputation for crooked numbers. For instance, which features of the industry cause the timing of production and marketing expenses to be less controversial? How has the evolution of account- ing standards for the entertainment industry influenced the financing of movie production and distribution?

The movie is then shipped out for domestic theatrical distribution, with "Theatrical Release and the Launching of Motion Pictures" by Charles C. Moul and Steven M. Shugan. The issues of when to release a movie and how to capitalize on (or minimize the effect of) word of mouth are perhaps the most overtly strategic questions in the industry's supply chain. What is the benefit of a summer or holiday release? How much of an impact do critics have on a movie's box-office performance? And what are the impacts of a director and starring cast on admissions, on advertising, and on the number of exhibiting theaters?

Jehoshua Eliashberg examines issues arising in theatrical exhibition with "The Film Exhibition Business: Critical Issues, Practice, and Re- search." The tasks of the multiplex operator have vastly increased as the number of screens within a single theater has expanded over the last twenty years. Of late, there have been additional concerns with the ex- pansion and contraction of theaters over the last ten years. Is the domestic exhibition sector yet at a sustainable level of capacity, or is more shake-out on the way? How will technology and changing market factors affect how movies are shown? And how large is the threat to theatrical exhibition posed by digital piracy?

The ancillary markets of foreign markets and video (especially DVD) are considered in Charles B. Weinberg's "Profits out of the Picture: Research Issues and Revenue Sources Beyond the North American Box Office." The industry continues to adapt to the fact that revenue from videotapes and videodiscs now far surpasses revenue from theatrical releases. But which aspects of a movie's domestic theatrical release carry over to consumers' decisions in the video market? How does a studio balance the benefits of these carried-over effects with the potential for videos cannibalizing theatrical admissions when choosing when to release a video? Do these answers inform our understanding of the relationship between the domestic and foreign markets?

It is our collective hope that this volume will facilitate and guide new research on the movie industry. To this end, it is my pleasure to acknowledge the following persons for their support of this work: Steve Smith, Melinda Warren, Christine Moseley, and Gloria Lucy of the Weidenbaum Center; Jeff Smith and Lloyd Silverman of Washington University Film and Media Studies; Morgan Rose for his research and editorial assistance; Christopher Allard for his editorial assistance; and, lastly, Dee Rader, whose boundless energy fueled this endeavor from its beginning to this conclusion.

# 1

# Critiquing Hollywood: The Political Economy of Motion Pictures

### JANET WASKO

Historically, motion pictures have been analyzed from many different perspectives and approaches. The business of film is receiving much closer scrutiny these days, again from diverse viewpoints. Although the popular press has always been fascinated with the spectacle of Hollywood, more media attention seems to be devoted these days to the business of film making in publications such as *Entertainment Weekly* and television programs such as *Entertainment Tonight*. Of course, much of this coverage is prompted by the industry itself through the studios' extensive publicity and promotion operations.

On the other hand, film industry insiders have produced a wide range of literature that more rigorously discusses the business practices of commercial film making in the United States. Many are aimed at Hollywood wannabes (for instance, Levy 2000), while others are mostly anecdotal essays about the industry (for instance, most anything by Peter Bart). At one time, Squire (1983, 1992) was one of the few sources that provided useful inside information on how the industry worked as a business. More recently, however, a number of industry accountants and legal experts have offered books detailing the complex financial and legal arrangements that surround the production, distribution, and retailing of commercial films (for instance, Daniels et al. 1998; Moore 2000). In addition, financial and investment advisors regularly produce detailed analysis, useful even for those not interested in investing in the industry (for instance, Vogel 2001; Cones 1996).

Closely related to these sources are the recent studies by economists representing mostly neoclassical economic approaches and using econometric analysis. While typically aiming to explain or predict the success or failure of films in various markets, a wide range of such studies has been produced over the last decade or so, some by authors represented in this volume.

Meanwhile, even as film critics and cinema-studies scholars continue to produce seemingly endless studies of individual films, stars, genres, and styles, more attention has been devoted to Hollywood as a business over the past decade or so. (More discussion of this work follows.)

Political economy represents a distinctly different approach to the study of film yet has not received much recognition within cinema studies or by other film analysts. This chapter presents an overview of this approach, including its roots in classic political economy and the application of political economy in communications and media studies. Examples of the political economic studies of film are discussed, as well as future directions for this research tradition.

## POLITICAL ECONOMY

The political economy of motion pictures is grounded in the general study of political economy, which draws on eighteenth-century Scottish enlightenment thinking and its critique in the nineteenth century. For Adam Smith, David Ricardo, and others, the study of economic issues was called *political economy* and was grounded in social theory. Further, political economy focused on the production, distribution, exchange, and consumption of wealth and the consequences for the welfare of individuals and society. More specifically, they studied one arrangement for the allocation of resources – they studied *capitalism* as a system of social production.

Classical political economy evolved as capitalism developed, adding Marx and Engels' historical materialism and class analysis in the nineteenth century, and emphasizing a radical critique of the evolving capitalist system through a moral stance in opposition to the unjust and inequitable characteristics of that system.

During the last half of the nineteenth century, however, there was a fundamental shift in the study of economic issues, as the focus changed from macro- to microanalysis. Emphasis was placed on individual rather than societal concerns, and the methods used came from the social sciences rather than from moral philosophy. These changes were represented in the basic shift in the name of the discipline – from *political economy* to *economics*.

Although neoclassical economics prevails today, political economy has survived in different forms. In communications studies, radical, critical, or Marxian political economy has been applied and has been recognized as a distinct tradition. In *The Political Economy of Communications*, Vincent Mosco has defined this version of political economy as "the study of the social relations, particularly power relations, that mutually constitute the production, distribution and consumption of resources" (Mosco 1996, p. 25). He explains that political economy is about survival and control, or how societies are organized to produce what is necessary to survive, and how order is maintained to meet societal goals. Mosco further delineates four central characteristics of critical political economy, which are helpful in understanding this approach:

1. *Social change and history.* Political economy continues the tradition of classic theorists, uncovering the dynamics of capitalism – its cyclical nature, the growth of monopoly capital, the state apparatus, and so forth.

2. *Social totality*: Political economy is a holistic approach which, in concrete terms, explores the relationship among commodities, institutions, social relations, and hegemony, exploring the determination among these elements, although some elements are stressed more than others.

3. *Moral philosophy*: Critical political economy also follows the classical theorists' emphasis on moral philosophy, including not only analysis of the economic system but also discussion of the policy problems and moral issues that arise from it. For some contemporary scholars, this is the distinguishing characteristic of political economy.

4. *Praxis*: Finally, political economists attempt to transcend the distinction between research and policy, orienting their work towards actual social change and practice or, as Marx pointed out: "Philosophers have sought to understand the system, the point is to change it."

Mosco's model draws strongly on the work of British political economists Graham Murdock and Peter Golding, who distinguished critical political economy from mainstream economics: it is holistic, historical, centrally concerned with the balance between capitalist enterprise and public intervention, and "goes beyond technical issues of efficiency to engage with basic moral questions of justice, equity and the public good" (Golding and Murdock 1991).

These explanations set the stage and provide the grounding for applying political economy to the study of communications and media, including motion pictures.

## POLITICAL ECONOMY APPLIED TO COMMUNICATIONS

The academic study of communications has not always embraced economic analysis, much less a political economic approach. During the 1940s and 1950s, communications scholars focused primarily on individual effects and psychologically oriented research, with little concern for the economic context in which media is produced, distributed, and consumed.

In the 1950s and early 1960s, former Federal Communications Commission (FCC) economist and University of Illinois professor Dallas Smythe urged scholars to consider communications as an important component of the economy and to understand it as an economic entity. In 1960, he presented one of the first applications of political economy to communications, defining the approach as the study of political policies and economic processes, their interrelations, and their mutual influence on social institutions (Smythe 1960). He argued that the central purpose of applying political economy to communications was to evaluate the effects of communications agencies in terms of the policies by which they are organized and operated or to study the structure and policies of communications institutions in their social settings. Smythe further delineated research questions emanating from policies of production, allocation, or distribution, and capital, organization, and control, concluding that the studies that might evolve from these areas were practically endless.

In the 1970s, Murdock and Golding (1974) defined political economy of communications as fundamentally interested in studying communications and media as commodities produced by capitalist industries. The article represented "a ground-breaking exercise . . . a conceptual map for a political economic analysis of the media where none existed in British literature" (Mosco 1996, p. 102). A later work (Murdock and Golding 1979) placed political economy within the broader framework of critical and Marxian theory, with links to the Frankfurt School, as well as to other critical theorists. Nicholas Garnham (1979) further outlined the approach, noting that the political economy of communications involves analyzing "the modes of cultural production and consumption developed within capitalist societies."

Media scholars studying political economy often draw on several disciplines – specifically history, economics, sociology, and political science. And, while some may question whether or not a specific methodology is involved, the study of political economy uses a wide range of techniques and methods, including not only Marxist economics but also methods utilized in history and sociology, especially power-structure research and institutional analysis.

Because historical analysis is mandatory, the approach is able to provide important insight into social change and movement. Political economy becomes crucial in order to document communications in its total social context. Interrelationships between media industries and sites of power in society are necessary for complete analysis, and their analysis helps to dispel some common myths about the economic and political system, especially notions of pluralism, free enterprise, competition, and so on. Through study of ownership and control, political economists analyze relations of power and confirm a class system and structural inequalities. In that the position includes economic *and* political analysis, it is therefore necessary grounding for ideological readings and cultural analysis. And, through identification of contradictions, political economic analysis provides strategies for intervention, resistance, and change.

## POLITICAL ECONOMY OF FILM

The U.S. film industry has been the focus of ongoing research by a few researchers in the political economy of communications. Thus, the political economy of film incorporates those characteristics that define political economy generally, as discussed previously, namely social change and history, social totality, moral grounding, and praxis.

Fundamentally, the political economy of film analyzes motion pictures as commodities produced and distributed within a capitalist industrial structure. As Pendakur notes, film as a commodity must be seen as a "tangible product and intangible service" (Pendakur 1990, pp. 39–40). Similar to other industry analyses, the approach addresses questions pertaining to market structure and performance. However, political economists analyze these issues as part of the larger communications and media industry and within a wider social context. Indeed, the focus on one medium or industry, such as film, may be seen as antithetical to political economy's attempt to go beyond merely describing the economic organization of the media industries.

The political and ideological implications of these economic arrangements are also relevant, as film must be placed within an entire social, economic, and political context and critiqued in terms of the contribution to maintaining and reproducing structures of power. The political economic study of film must involve not only a description of the industry, but also as Mosco explains, "a theoretical understanding of these developments, situating them within a wider capitalist totality encompassing class and other social relations offering a sustained critique from a moral evaluative position" (Mosco 1996, p. 115).

Some of the key distinctions between political economy and other models are the recognition and critique of the uneven distribution of power and wealth represented by the industry, the attention paid to labor issues, the role of the State, the alternatives to commercial film, and the attempts to challenge the industry rather than accepting the status quo. For instance, why are Hollywood films popular with audiences all over the world? Some might argue that American films are just better than other nations' productions. Rather than celebrating Hollywood's success, political economists are interested in how U.S. films came to dominate international film markets, what mechanisms are in place to sustain such market dominance, how the State becomes involved in this process, how the export of film is related to marketing of other media products, the consequences for indigenous film industries in other countries, and the political/cultural implications.

For a political economist, Hollywood works as an industry that manufactures and markets commodities. Although these commodities are often engaging and exciting entertainment products, it is still important to understand the process by which they are produced and distributed. The process involves film concepts that become film commodities, passing through the production, distribution, and exhibition/retail stages. Most recently, Hollywood films have become more commercial through product placement, as well as spawning new commodities such as merchandise and other media products.

Political economists are especially interested in these developments, as well as the corporations that control the industry – the Hollywood majors. These companies are part of diversified entertainment conglomerates that operate at a global level, producing and distributing a range of products and constantly searching for new markets. Though the majors dominate domestic and global markets, their products do not simply compete with other commodities in these marketplaces but are protected and defended through various strategies that rely on the State.

Thus, a political economy of film is concerned not only with the structure of the film industry and the prevailing vertical and horizontal integration that has historically characterized the industry. Analysis also must include an understanding of the interaction between the industry and the State, both in domestic and international markets, including the enforcement (or lack of enforcement) of regulations (such as antitrust), intellectual property rights, and the like.

Hollywood has always had a proclivity towards integration and concentration. Indeed, one industry observer concluded that Hollywood suffers from "chronic monopoly" (Borneman 1976). By the 1920s, a handful of corporations dominated the industry through their ownership of production and distribution companies, as well as major theater chains around the country (see Huettig 1944). In addition to this integration, several anticompetitive tactics were standard industry practices through the end of the 1940s. "Block-booking" was the name given to the studio practice that bundled two or more films for licensing in a single market. In other words, a distributor demands that an exhibitor accept a less desirable film (or films) before accepting a bid on a highly desirable film. Distributors also often requested bids for films without providing exhibitors the opportunity to view the film, a practice called "blind-bidding."

Finally, distributors typically required that exhibitors charge a minimum admissions price, a practice that is illegal.

In light of these concerns, the U.S. film industry has had a long history of antitrust activity. Numerous challenges to the majors' anticompetitive practices were waged from the 1920s, especially by independent theater owners. However, serious changes did not come about until the government's antitrust case against the Hollywood majors in the early 1940s, resulting in a series of consent decrees in the late 1940s/early 1950s. The "Paramount decrees" forced vertical disintegration of the industry after the five major studio-distributors (the "Big Five") were found guilty of restraint of trade including vertical and horizontal price fixing (see Conant 1960). Certain trade practices (such as block-booking and admissions price fixing) were declared illegal and the majors were forced to divorce their theater operations. Although the action was called a "triumph for antitrust," it might be argued that the ultimate result was beneficial for the majors, setting the stage for the "new" production–distribution companies to diversify into the newly emerging business of television, leaving the ailing exhibition sector of the industry to fend for itself. Since the Paramount decrees, several other new media outlets (home video, cable, etc.) have been embraced by the majors with few challenges from the government. Indeed, the government has facilitated the current integration and concentration in the media/entertainment industry with little enforcement of antitrust regulations. Chapter 5 details this integration within the exhibition sector.

Although the government is sometimes seen as an impediment to business, some government policies have especially favored the motion picture industry. For instance, the major film corporations were the beneficiaries when the FCC implemented the Financial Interest and Syndication Rules (or Fin-Syn) in 1970. In an attempt to increase program diversity and limit the market control of the three broadcast television networks, the rules prohibited network participation in the financial interest of the television programs they aired beyond first-run exhibition and the creation of in-house syndication arms, especially in the domestic market. The Hollywood majors profited handsomely from the sale of television programming until the regulations eventually were dropped around 1991. Since then, the major film corporations have become part of enormous vertically integrated entertainment conglomerates that now own not only the major television networks, but also cable networks, video stores, and (some) theaters, as well as producing and distributing entertainment commodities for these outlets.

It also is important to understand that the Hollywood majors' trade association, the Motion Picture Association of America (MPAA), strongly promotes these favorable State policies. The organization aggressively lobbies the U.S. government for domestic favors and protection, fighting everything from unfavorable trade policies to copyright infringement and First Amendment issues. In addition, the Hollywood majors operate globally through an export cartel, the Motion Picture Association (MPA), often referred to as "the Little State Department." The MPA is especially active in clearing the way for the international sales of Hollywood products through various strategies, including direct trade negotiations with foreign governments, antipiracy campaigns, and so on.

Generally, then, a critical political economy of film insists that the Hollywood majors dominate domestic and global film markets not simply by competing with other companies in the marketplace, but also with deliberate attempts to gain protection and assistance from the State.

Along with analyzing and critiquing this process, a political economy of film challenges a few of the assumptions that are often made about the film business by analysts and insiders. A few of these illusions are summarized briefly here to illustrate some of the issues that have been considered by political economists analyzing the U.S. film industry.[1]

---

[1]  The discussion that follows is based on Wasko (2003).

## Illusion #1: "There's No Business Like Show Business."

Some economists and other industry observers insist that film production and distribution is a unique and risky business. However, both of these assumptions need to be considered more carefully.

Although the U.S. film industry may have some unique characteristics, it is still an industry organized around profit. From a film's inception as an idea or concept to its distribution to a wide range of outlets and locations, film industry insiders explain that the motivating force is the bottom line. Furthermore, even though each product may be singular and unique, the techniques and strategies that are used to produce and promote Hollywood films are comparable to other industries. In other words, an industrial process is in place that does not always appear to be peculiar or unusual.

Whereas film production and distribution is consistently claimed to be a risky business, much of the "risk" has been introduced and sustained by the industry itself. Expensive blockbuster, star-studded features pro-moted by massive marketing campaigns are characteristic of Hollywood's attempt to attract massive box-office revenues, as well as to build further profits from subsequent distribution outlets. These skyrocketing costs are one of the main reasons why Hollywood filmmaking is said to be risky.

But is the film business actually as risky a business as that? A common assumption is that Hollywood films rarely return their investments at the box office and companies survive from the successes of a few blockbuster films. This assumption, however, belies that fact that box-office receipts are not the only source of income for film commodities. The U.S. box office is only the beginning of a chain of windows or markets where little additional investment is needed but more income and, not infre-quently, extensive profits are produced. For example: The highly pub-licized "failure," *Waterworld*, received only $88 million at U.S. theaters; however, the film went on to garner more than $255 million at box offices worldwide. One estimate of the film's overall receipts was $350 million, which would include ancillary markets. More recent examples might be DreamWorks' *Spirit: Stallion of the Cimarron*, which earned about $73 million in U.S. theaters but more than $120 million from DVD and video sales and rentals. Also, *Atlantis: The Lost Empire* attracted only $84 million in theaters, but video and DVD sales and rentals grossed about $132 million. Chapter 6 includes many additional examples and insights into how this has changed the industry.

For the film industry, more distribution outlets have translated into less risk. Videocassette, DVD, and cable release have provided especially lucrative rewards for films that do well in theaters, as well as giving "legs" to films that have not performed well in theatrical release. Moreover, globalization and privatization have opened international markets that further reduce the risk of distributing these infinitely exportable products. Obviously, these factors must be taken into account when considering the claim that Hollywood's business is uniquely risky.

## Illusion #2: "It's a Dog-Eat-Dog Business."

Some claim that the industry is heavily competitive. However, it is obvious by looking at the breakdown of market shares for the retail outlets where feature films are bought and sold that Hollywood represents a concentrated industry. From the theatrical box office, to VHS and DVD sales, to the sale of films to television and cable outlets, the Hollywood majors rule the film business as a reigning oligopoly. Although there may be some competition (for instance, between major releases), the studios also cooperate in typical oligopolistic fashion to determine industry policies and to protect and promote the industry.

This dominance is echoed in the clout that is demonstrated in the various deals that characterize the industry – power deals that involve the major studios and Hollywood's power players, with little room for independents or smaller companies to compete for talent or other resources. The majors' strength can be contrasted to an independent company that only produces films and, thus, is unable to capitalize or draw strength from diversified revenues or from a conglomerate owner.

Although the film industry accommodates independent production, the majors ultimately set the agenda and reap the bulk of the rewards. Through their control over film distribution, as well as pursuing various strategies to reduce risk and protect and promote their products, the Hollywood majors have maintained their dominance of the U.S. film industry, as well as much of the world's film business.

## Illusion #3: ". . . a Supremely Democratic Form of Entertainment."

A film executive once described the industry as democratic because "customers vote for one movie over another by simply putting down hard cash" (Squire 1992, p. 24). Another assumption about Hollywood is that the industry offers a wide range of entertainment choices that are determined by audience demand.

Although hundreds of films are produced and distributed each year, it may be possible to argue that audience choice is still somewhat constrained in various ways. Hollywood consistently distributes formulaic and recycled products to theaters and other outlets that crave these kinds of products. Despite the artistic claims made by some film makers, Hollywood films are made because they are perceived to be profitable or represent low risk. Thus, certain kinds of films are made more often than others, such as genre films that appeal to a young audience, remakes and sequels, formula films featuring well-known stars, and so on. One of the points to be made here is that many segments of the movie audience may not be served by typical Hollywood fare. For instance, older audience members may be uninterested in the typical selection of films at their local theaters and thus opt more often for televised entertainment.

But it is also possible to argue that audiences' preferences don't matter as much as is typically assumed. Even though audiences are said to influence the films that are produced and distributed, such influence is mainly a matter of choosing between the films that are actually made available. Certainly, much of American popular culture (including Hollywood films) is mass produced in this way. In other words, it is not created by public preference but by industrial intentions. In this sense, the claim of Hollywood as a "democratic form of entertainment" may be somewhat overstated.

## Illusion #4: "That's Entertainment!"

Serious discussions of the film industry are often met with a typical response: "Well, it's only entertainment." Despite this commonly held assumption, it must be insisted that Hollywood is not just about entertainment. As we have seen, it's a business that produces and distributes products that have significant economic, political, and cultural implications. Hollywood films may offer engaging fantasies and convenient escape from the drudgeries of daily life, but they also offer explicit visions of the world and lessons for living in that world. In addition to their obvious economic importance, motion pictures are ideological products and thus are socially and politically significant as well. Consequently, understanding how Hollywood works is a necessary component to discerning film's overall social significance.

## Corporate Hollywood

Hollywood seems to thrive on myths and illusions, even those that pertain to the business of film. These illusions become more problematic on closer inspection of how the industry actually works. Indeed, several general economic trends are alive and well in Hollywood. As with many other capitalist industries, the processes of concentration, commodification, and commercialization currently govern the U.S. film industry.

Furthermore, the industry contributes to the growing trend of consumerism that dominates Western societies through the ceaseless manufacture of redundant merchandise.

Of course, the megacorporations that dominate the entertainment world are not invincible. Challenges abound, from the potential competition posed by new technologies to ongoing threats from intellectual property infringement. Furthermore, there are no guarantees that Hollywood companies or players will always make the correct decisions to ensure their survival. After all, Hollywood must still depend on the ability to attract audiences, as well as sometimes hostile politicians and other political and economic vagaries. Ultimately, their own grand plans may prove fatal, as sometimes predicted when considering the constantly increasing costs of talent and the continually expanding budgets for major Hollywood films.

Yet, with the enhanced need for product to feed new technologies and expanding entertainment markets, the Hollywood majors remain poised and ready to supply it. Although the majors already receive income from diverse resources, new distribution outlets mean even further profits. The industry has continued its predilection for integrating production, distribution, and retail outlets, maintaining its control over these new resources. In addition, the majors have built alliances with other companies as well as developing interdependencies between old and new technologies. And, again, they have worked to ensure relaxed government regulation and a supportive State, thus merging into large synergistic corporations that control huge chunks of popular cultural production, not only in the United States but also around the world.

In other words, the majors – bolstered by being owned by global entertainment conglomerates – are well positioned to maintain their prominence, not only in the traditional film industry but also in new forms of entertainment, as well as in the culture industry as a whole. Currently, that means selling film commodities in new formats such as DVD, the

Internet, and video-on-demand; commercializing films through product placements; creating new commodities through merchandising; and expanding into global markets. Although the technologies and the players may change, and the strategies used to promote and protect the film business may shift in subtle ways, the motives are likely to remain the same.

Thus, it also seems likely that understanding how Hollywood works as an industry, producing and distributing commodities within a more general capitalist system, will remain an important requirement for understanding motion pictures in the twenty-first century. A political economic analysis is one of the approaches that help with this kind of understanding.

## CONTRAST TO OTHER APPROACHES

Before discussing some of the work by political economists in film, it may be helpful to contrast this approach to two other areas of research that sometimes focus on the business of Hollywood.

## Media Economics

Film is a form of mediated communications, thus appropriate for many of the approaches used in studying other forms of media. It also is necessary, then, to mention another approach to studying the business of motion pictures – that is, *media economics*. As mentioned previously, more specific attention to economics has been evident in the field of communications and media studies during the last decade, with scholars identifying media economics as a distinct focus of research activity. Examples include texts by Robert Picard (1989), Alan Albarron (1996), and Allison Alexander et al. (1993), as well as the *Journal of Media Economics*, which was introduced in 1988. The goal of the journal, as stated in its

Contributor Information section, is "...to broaden understanding and discussion of the impact of economic and financial activities on media operations and managerial decisions." Generally, these media economics texts and the journal echo the concerns of mainstream (neoclassical) economics. As the journal's first editor explains:

> Media economics is concerned with how media operators meet the informational and entertainment wants and needs of audiences, advertisers and society with available resources. It deals with the factors influencing production of media goods and services and the allocation of those products for consumption. (Picard 1989, p. 7)

For the most part, the emphasis of media economics is on microeconomic issues rather than macroanalysis and focuses primarily on producers and consumers in media markets. Typically, the concern is how media industries and companies can succeed, prosper, or move forward. Whereas competition may be assessed, little emphasis is placed on questions of ownership or the implications of concentrated ownership and control. Again, these approaches emphasize description (or "what is") rather than critique (or "what ought to be").

## Cinema Studies

In the late 1970s, Thomas Guback wrote an essay entitled "Are We Looking at the Right Things in Film?" in which he argued that the academic study of cinema focused overwhelmingly on criticism and theory, with a dash of atheoretical history (Guback 1978). Guback's main point was that film studies typically neglected the analysis of cinema as an economic institution and as a medium of communication. It is clear that much more economic analysis has been done in film studies since Guback's critique in the 1970s. Generally, economic approaches to film can still be characterized as Allen and Gomery (1985) did in their discussion of economic film history. Allen and Gomery favor the *institutional* or *industrial organizational model*, as described by Douglas Gomery:

> The industrial organization model of structure, conduct, and per-
> formance provides a powerful and useful analytical framework for
> economic analysis. Using it, the analyst seeks to define the size and
> scope of the structure of an industry and then go on to examine its
> economic behavior. Both of these steps require analyzing the status
> and operations of the industry, not as the analyst wishes it were.
> Evaluation of its performance is the final step, a careful weighing of
> "what is" versus "what ought to be." (Gomery 1989, p. 58)

Examples of an industrial analysis include Gomery's early work on
the introduction of sound, followed by studies of exhibition, and the like.
More recently, Justin Wyatt's analysis of "high concept" as a dominant
force in contemporary Hollywood draws directly on industrial organization economics (Wyatt 1994, pp. 65–66). Much of the work in edited
collections on the film industry more or less explicitly follows an industrial model (see Balio [1976]; Kindem [1982]).

The recognition of the importance of this kind of work was indicated in the announcement of the theme for the 1999 Society for Cinema
Studies (SCS) conference: "Media Industries: Past, Present & Future." It
indicated, first, how media beyond film have been integrated into previously exclusively *cinema* studies but also the recognition of the importance of economic and industry issues. The conference description read
as follows:

> Topics for panels and papers might include media industry is-
> sues concerning production, distribution and exhibition, regula-
> tory parameters, the relationship between technological change and
> industrial structure, international industry comparisons, institu-
> tional/industrial issues concerning independent, and alternative me-
> dia and *studies in political economy of the mass media*. (Emphasis
> added) (from SCS website)

Although there was still little evidence of much political economic
research at this particular conference, it seems that a growing number of

young film scholars at least are beginning to integrate this approach into their work, as discussed in the next section.

### EXAMPLES OF STUDIES REPRESENTING POLITICAL ECONOMY OF FILM

The political economy of film is represented in a wide range of research. Some classic economic studies fit the previous description but were not explicitly identified with political economy. For instance, Klingender and Legg's *Money Behind the Screen* examined finance capital in the film industry in 1937, tracing studio owners and their capitalist backers (Klingender and Legg 1937), whereas Mae Huettig's study of the film industry in the late 1930s documented the power inherent in the various sectors of the industry (Huettig 1944). In addition, Michael Conant's (1960) study of antitrust in the film industry remains a valuable foundation to understanding the industry's structure and relationship with the State.

More recently, Guback's work represents an ideal example of political economy of film. *The International Film Industry* presented primary documentation about how the U.S. domination of European film industries intensified after 1945, with the direct assistance of the U.S. government (Guback 1969). He followed this classic study with several articles documenting the international extension of U.S. film companies in the 1970s and 1980s, especially emphasizing the role of the State in these activities (in Balio 1976). In another article, Guback defended a nation's right to resist Hollywood's domination and develop its own film industry based on economic and cultural factors (Guback 1989). And, finally, in an in-depth outline of the U.S. film industry in *Who Owns the Media?*, Guback presented a strong critique of Hollywood's structure and practices, as opposed to the other industrially oriented articles in the same volume (Compaine 1982).

Pendakur's study of the Canadian film industry employs a radical political economy of film but also incorporates industrial organization theory to examine the market structure of Canadian film (Pendakur 1990). "Marxian political economy's concern with power in class societies and its emphasis on a dialectical view of history help explain how the battle to create an indigenous film industry has been fought in Canada, in whose interests, and with what outcome" (p. 39). Pendakur (1998) also examined labor issues in film, adding to the growing literature documenting the history of labor organizations and workers in the U.S. film industry. His most recent work is a look at the film industry in India (Pendakur 2003).

Meanwhile, many other scholars have taken a political economic approach in looking at various aspects of film. Nicholas Garnham incorporated an analysis of the "Economics of the U.S. Motion Picture Industry" to exemplify the production of culture in his collection, *Capitalism and Communications* (Garnham 1990). Aksoy and Robins' more recent study of the motion picture industry focuses on issues on concentration and globalization and draws fundamentally on political economy (Aksoy and Robins 1992). Another example is Prindle's *Risky Business: The Political Economy of Hollywood*, which especially emphasizes the social and political implications of Hollywood's unique industrial structure (Prindle 1993). Most recently, Miller et al. (2001) have presented an overview of global Hollywood, relying strongly on a critical political economic approach and emphasizing the role of film workers. Other important work that embraces political economy includes Frederick Wasser's (2001) study of video, Ron Bettig's (1996) work on copyright, and Michael Nielsen's research on film labor (Nielsen 1985, Nielsen and Mailles 1995).[2]

In my own work, I have examined capital, technology, and labor as they pertain to Hollywood. *Movies and Money* (Wasko 1982) presented the historical development of relationships between Hollywood and financial institutions, while *Hollywood in the Information Age* (Wasko 1994)

---

[2] Interestingly, all of these scholars, as well as the author, were students of Tom Guback's.

examined continuity and change in the U.S. film industry relating the introduction of new technologies during the 1980s and early 1990s. In addition, "Hollywood Meets Madison Avenue" considered the ongoing commercialization of film by focusing on growth of product placement, tie-ins, and merchandising activities in film marketing (Wasko, Phillips, and Purdie 1993), while an overview of Hollywood labor unions was presented in a collection on global media production (Wasko 1998). Finally, *How Hollywood Works* (2003) describes the Hollywood film commodity from its inception to its sale in retail markets.

## CHALLENGES TO A POLITICAL ECONOMY OF FILM

Despite these various studies, it still might be argued that political economy is much less common in film studies than in communications research. If so, then why? It is possible that Guback's explanations in the essay mentioned previously are still relevant. Scholars depend on the material that is available for study, whether that is film texts or industry-supplied information. Although more media attention has been focused on the film industry through stories and programs that examine the making of films and box-office numbers, it is mostly coverage generated by the industry itself and hardly critical. Indeed, it is still a challenge to find reliable and relevant data about the film industry. For instance, where can one find accurate production figures beyond the public relations rumor mill reported in *Variety* or other trade publications? Where is it possible to find accurate or meaningful figures on stock ownership?

The type of information that is available may lend itself especially well to congratulatory coverage of the industry's triumphs. But it also might be argued that much scholarly writing on the industry resists any challenges to the status quo. Even when information is available, the commercial and profit-motivated goals of the industry are rarely questioned, but assumed.

On the other hand, one might also wonder why film is less often in-cluded in much of the work in political economy of communications. Although film appears in general overviews of the communications or media industries, it seems to receive less careful analysis than other forms of media or communications (see Jowett and Linton 1980). One obvious reason may be the academic fragmentation that still sometimes separates film studies from media and communications studies in university or-ganizational charts, professional organizations, and scholarly journals. Film studies typically have been based in the humanities, whereas com-munications and media studies tend to draw more on the social sciences. Beyond this fragmentation, there may also be differences in the percep-tion of film's importance to communications scholars. Film sometimes still represents "only entertainment," thus not as worthy of scholarly attention as news and information programming or computer and in-formation technologies.

But these oversights need to be addressed if we are to understand film in its actual social context. These days, film *must* be considered as part of communications and media industry. More than ever before, distribution outlets such as cable and satellite services link news, information, and entertainment programs; and, sometime in the future, it seems likely that there will be further links via new digital and multimedia forms. It is no longer novel to observe that news is looking more like entertainment, with new forms evolving, such as infotainment, docudramas, and so forth.

But, importantly, these activities are, more than ever, under the same corporate ownership. The same companies that are involved with other media and communications activities produce films, and it is no secret that fewer and fewer giant corporations control these activities. These multinational corporations have diversified into all areas of the me-dia, sometimes attempting to maximize profitability by building synergy between their corporate divisions. For some of these companies, film plays a key role in these synergistic efforts, as corporations such as the Walt Disney Company build product lines which begin with a film but continue through television, cable, publishing, theme parks, merchandising, and so on. These days, companies like Disney not only distribute products to these outlets but also own the outlets.

Although the expansion of global markets may be relatively new for some media, the U.S. film industry developed global marketing techniques as early as the 1920s and continues its dominant position in international media markets today. Communications researchers might at least be interested in looking more closely at the international expansion of the U.S. film industry to better understand the historical evolution of globalization.

## NEW DIRECTIONS FOR POLITICAL ECONOMY

Even though there is a steadily growing body of literature that analyzes film from a political economic perspective, more attention is needed in various areas. Obviously, new technologies are constantly presenting new possibilities for the industry and demand analysis by scholars (see Harries 2002).

In addition, political economic analysis can become more effective by linking with other compatible approaches. It is apparent to many political economists that cultural studies, whether centered on film or other areas, offer important insights that are crucial to understanding the reception of film and its ideological significance. As critical film analysts come to an awareness of the significance of political economic grounding, productive links might be made to integrate research, policy efforts, and other practical activities.

Political economists have been accused of ignoring film audiences. Hagen and Wasko (2000) deal with this issue in a volume that includes both reception analysts and political economists discussing issues relating to audiences and consumption.

Other links need to be forged with researchers who share similar political commitments. For instance, political economy has neglected many of the issues posed by feminist theorists, who have been quite active in cinema studies. A collection by Meehan and Riordan (2001) specifically addresses this blind spot and promises to make an important contribution to forging these links.

Although the political economy of film may not have received as much recognition in the past, the future may be different as more scholars engage in research that embraces this approach. Whether or not this offers a real challenge to the industry, however, is another question. Importantly, critiquing the industry is only one facet of a political economy of film. Effectively challenging the industry as well as envisioning realistic alternatives to the current industrial arrangements are challenges that political economists face in the future. In other words, attention needs to be given to "what ought to be" as well as to "what is." Nevertheless, as the film industry and its wealth become ever more concentrated, it is increasingly difficult to avoid the issues and analysis that a political economy of film currently presents.

### REFERENCES

Aksoy, Asuand, and Kevin Robins. 1992. "Hollywood for the 21st Century: Global Competition for Critical Mass in Image Markets," *Cambridge Journal of Economics* 16(1): 1–22.

Albarran, Alan B. 1996. *Media Economics: Understanding Markets, Industries, and Concepts*, Ames, IA: Iowa State University Press.

Alexander, Alison, James Owers, and Rodney Carveth, eds. 1993. *Media Economics: Theory and Practice*, Hillsdale, NJ: L. Erlbaum Associates.

Allen, Robert C., and Douglas Gomery. 1985. *Film History: Theory and Practice*, New York: Alfred A. Knopf.

Balio, Tino, ed. 1976. *The American Film Industry*, Madison, WI: University of Wisconsin Press.

Bettig, Ron. 1996. *Copyrighting Culture: The Political Economy of Intellectual Property*, Boulder, CO: Westview Press.

Borneman, Ernest. 1976. "United States versus Hollywood. The Case Study of an Antitrust Suit," in *The American Film Industry*, Tino Balio (ed.), Madison, WI: University of Wisconsin Press, S.332–70.

Compaine, Ben, ed. 1982. *Who Owns the Media? Concentration of Ownership in the Mass Communications Industry*, White Plains, NY: Knowledge Industry Publications.

Conant, Michael. 1960. *Antitrust in the Motion Picture Industry; Economic and Legal Analysis*, Berkeley, CA: University of California Press.

Cones, John W. 1996. *The Feature Film Distribution Deal: A Critical Analysis of the Single Most Important Film Industry Agreement*, Carbondale, IL: Southern Illinois University Press.

Daniels, Bill, David Leedy, and Steven D. Sills. 1998. *Movie Money: Understanding Hollywood's (Creative) Accounting Practices*, Los Angeles, CA: Silman-James Press.

Garnham, Nicholas. 1979. "Contribution to a Political Economy of Mass Communication," *Media, Culture and Society* 1: 123–46.

———. 1990. *Capitalism and Communications: Global Culture and the Economics of Information*, London: Sage Publications.

Golding, Peter, and Graham Murdock. 1991. "Culture, Communication, and Political Economy," in James Curran and Michael Gurevitch (eds.), *Mass Media and Society*, London: Edward Arnold, pp. 11–30.

Gomery, Douglas. 1989. "Media Economics: Terms of Analysis," *Critical Studies in Mass Communications* 6(1): 43–60.

———. 1969. *The International Film Industry: Western Europe and America Since 1945*, Bloomington, IN: Indiana University Press.

———. 1978. "Are We Looking at the Right Things in Film?," Society for Cinema Studies conference, Philadelphia, PA.

———. 1989. "Should a Nation Have Its Own Film Industry?" *Directions* 3(1): 489–92.

Hagen, Ingunn, and Janet Wasko. 2000. *Consuming Audiences? Production and Reception in Media Research*, Cresskill, NJ: Hampton Press.

Harries, Dan, ed. 2002. *The New Media Book*, London: BFI Publishing.

Huettig, Mae D. 1944. *Economic Control of the Motion Picture Industry*, Philadelphia, PA: University of Pennsylvania Press.

Jowett, Garth, and James M. Linton. 1980. *Movies as Mass Communications*, Beverly Hills, CA: Sage Publications.

Kindem, Gorham, ed. 1982. *The American Movie Industry: The Business of Motion Pictures*, Carbondale, IL: Southern Illinois Press.

Klingender, Francis D., and Stuart Legg. 1937. *Money Behind the Screen*, London: Lawrence & Wishart.

Levy, Frederick. 2000. *Hollywood 101: The Film Industry*, Los Angeles, CA: Renaissance Books.

Meehan, Eileen R., and Ellen Riordan. 2001. *Sex and Money: Feminism and Political Economy in the Media*, Minneapolis, MN: University of Minnesota Press.

Miller, Toby, Nitin Govil, John McMurria, and Richard Maxwell. 2001. *Global Hollywood*, London: BFI Publishing.

Moore, Schuyler M. 2000. *The Biz: The Basic Business, Legal and Financial Aspects of the Film Industry*, Los Angeles, CA: Silman-James Press.

Mosco, Vincent. 1996. *The Political Economy of Communications: Rethinking and Renewal*, London: Sage Publications.

Murdock, Graham, and Peter Golding. 1974. "For a Political Economy of Mass Communications," *Socialist Register*, 205–34.

———. 1979. "Capitalism, Communication and Class Relations," in James Curran, Michael Gurevitch, and Janet Woollacott (eds.), *Mass Communication and Society*, Beverly Hills, CA: Sage Publications.

Nielsen, Mike. 1985. *Motion Picture Craft Workers and Craft Unions in Hollywood: The Studio Era, 1912–1948*, Ph.D. dissertation, University of Illinois.

Nielsen, Mike, and Gene Mailes. 1995. *Hollywood's Other Blacklist: Union Struggles in the Studio System*, London: British Film Institute.

Pendakur, Manjunath. 1990. *Canadian Dreams and American Control: The Political Economy of the Canadian Film Industry*, Detroit, MI: Wayne State University.

———. 1998. "Hollywood North: Film and TV Production in Canada," in Gerald Sussman and John A. Lent (eds.), *Global Productions: Labor in the Making of the "Information Society,"* Cresskill, NJ: Hampton Press.

———. 2003. *Indian Popular Cinema: Industry, Ideology, and Consciousness*, Cresskill, NJ: Hampton Press.

Picard, Robert G. 1989. *Media Economics: Concepts and Issues*, Newbury Park, CA: Sage Publications.

Prindle, David F. 1993. *Risky Business: The Political Economy of Hollywood*, Boulder, CO: Westview Press.

Smythe, Dallas W. 1960. "On the Political Economy of Communication," *Journalism Quarterly*, Autumn, 563–72.

Society for Cinema Studies website (1999). http://www.cinstudies.org/99conf/Program.htm.

Squire, Jason E., ed. 1983, 1992. *The Movie Business Book*, New York: Simon and Schuster.

Vogel, Harold L. 2001. *Entertainment Industry Economics: A Guide for Financial Analysis*, 5th ed. New York: Cambridge University Press.

Wasko, Janet. 1982. *Movies and Money: Financing the American Film Industry*, Norwood, NJ: Ablex Publishing.

———. 1994. *Hollywood in the Information Age: Beyond the Silver Screen*, Cambridge: Polity Press.

———. 1998. "Challenges to Hollywood's Labor Force in the 1990s," Gerald Sussman and John A. Lent (eds.), *Global Productions: Labor in the Making of the "Information Society,"* Cresskill, NJ: Hampton Press.

———. 2003. *How Hollywood Works*, London: Sage Publications.

Wasko, Janet, Mark Phillips, and Chris Purdie. 1993. "Hollywood Meets Madison Ave.: The Commercialization of US Films," *Media, Culture and Society* 15(2).

Wasser, Frederick. 2001. *Veni, Vidi, Video: The Hollywood Empire and the VCR*, Austin, TX: University of Texas Press.

Wyatt, Justin. 1994. *High Concept: Movies and Marketing in Hollywood*, Austin, TX: University of Texas Press.

## 2

# Film Production in the Digital Age – What Do We Know about the Past and the Future?

### S. ABRAHAM RAVID

Film production is a fascinating process. A raw idea is crystallized into a full-blown production with characters, set, and story. Film projects are also very expensive commodities by any standard – the average film produced in 2002 cost $58.8 million dollars, with print and advertising costs north of $30 million (see www.mpaa.org).

Sometimes film development and production are on a fast track. In other cases, the route to production may take a very long time. For example, in 1995 the acclaimed historical novelist Patrick O'Brian met in Hollywood with Charlton Heston and Samuel Goldwyn Jr. to discuss how his literary work could be translated into the language of film. Even though his books had been extremely successful, it took eight years (during which time Mr. O'Brian passed away) for the books to be turned into "*Master and Commander: The Far Side of the World,*" released in December 2003.[1]

Such a long and uncertain process is not very common in other industries, except for industries facing regulatory hurdles and/or requiring a long research and development process. In particular, one may be able to

---

[1] *Weekly Variety*, August 25–31, 2003, front page.

draw comparisons with the biotechnology and drug industries, which face both regulatory hurdles and a long development process with uncertain prospects.[2]

In the studio era, which ended gradually with the Paramount decision in the late 1940s, studios controlled the entire decision process.[3] Since then, the development process has become much more diffuse, with many ways in which films can come into existence. There is still the traditional studio process, whereby a studio develops, produces, and distributes the film, and then there are many other ways – independent producers may independently finance the film and then seek a distributor who buys the completed product, or studios and small production companies may finance projects together with various possible arrangements. As of late 2003, there was consideration of an IPO for a company that would produce a single film and then liquidate.[4] In recent years, co-financing has become the rule rather than the exception in film financing (see Palia, Ravid, and Reisel 2003; Goettler and Leslie 2003).

Academic interest in the production process has centered on several issues. First is the issue of profitability. Can the economic success of a film be predicted based on any *ex ante* observed characteristics? Put differently, are there any observables that have a significant impact on either revenues or profits? This issue ties directly to the literature on stars, who are ubiquitous in films and in other creative industries.[5] Do stars create value, or are they expensive public relations gimmicks?

A second focus has been on the contracts governing the production process. Ignoring the contractual reality may lead one to miss the boat, making reasonable decisions look silly. Some contracts in the film

---

[2] Landers and Lublin (2003) describe how Merck's bet on research had come up short as four of eleven drugs long in development had already failed and two others had been delayed.

[3] See Litman (1998), Caves (2000), or Vogel (2001) for a description of the economics of the studio era.

[4] Barker (2003) discusses the case of Billy Dead Inc.

[5] For the classic article on this issue, see Rosen (1981); and also Adler (1985), MacDonald (1988), and Hamlen (1991).

industry, such as a pay-or-play contract, are quite different from contracts in other industries.

The other interesting feature of the film industry is the project-by-project nature of the contracts – in general, a team is assembled, a project is created, and then the team is dispersed and a new team assembles for the next project. Unlike other industries, the results of the project, both from a creative and from a financial point of view, are rather transparent (movie accounting notwithstanding). Therefore, hiring decisions can be based on a string of projects (see John, Ravid, and Sunder 2003).

I begin by discussing the profitability literature and then examine decision strategies by film executives and their implications. Next to be considered are contracting issues. Finally, I briefly suggest what digitalization implies for film production.

## STARS AND PROFITABILITY[6]

Profitability studies have been closely related to the study of stars. Stars have always been a puzzling phenomenon. Some stars seem to have vastly superior talents, whereas many others do not seem very different in looks or any other observable characteristic from many other talented performers. Yet, they receive vastly more attention, money, and recognition than anybody else.

Rosen (1981) formulated a classic model, which can presumably explain how small differences in quality can result in a star system, which rewards a few people disproportionately. Each consumer invests time, selects a level of quality and exposure (say, a number of records, videos, or DVDs to buy), and pays a certain amount (fixed for a level of quality). One would expect that consumers should be willing to pay disproportionately more for higher talent. This "bias towards superior talent" forms the demand side of the equation. However, even if this is not the case, a star phenomenon can occur if the supply is properly structured.

---

[6] Some of the material here is summarized in Ravid (2004).

There are economies of scale in production as well. A live performance for five thousand people does not cost much more than a live
performance for four thousand people and, for recorded and broadcast
performances, the marginal cost per customer is virtually zero. Because
the marginal cost of production is low, top talent may not charge much
more per ticket than less talented performers. Thus, viewers get a "bar-
gain" – much greater talent for only slightly more money. Top stars will
attract disproportionately larger audiences and collect much higher economic rents. This logic seems to apply to film production.[7]

Adler (1985) suggests that once consumers invest time in studying
stars, they tend to stay with them. His model does not even need quality
differentials to create superstars. MacDonald (1988) expands this setup
to a dynamic context, suggesting that in a two-period world, star pay is a
compensation for the skewed nature of success in this business.

In the movie business, one talks about "bankable stars" who can
"open" a movie. In many cases, stars are able to make projects happen.
The question is whether or not this perception is based on economic
reality.[8]

There have been a few early studies of the determinants of profitability
in movies. Litman (1983) finds that Academy Award nominations or
winnings are significantly related to revenues. Smith and Smith (1986)
analyze a sample that includes only the most successful films in the 1950s,
'60s, and '70s. The results (which differ by decade) of running revenues
against awards are curious. For instance, winning an award seems to have
a negative and significant effect in the 1960s and a positive and significant
effect in the 1970s. The Best Actor award variable is insignificant, whereas
the Best Actress award variable changes sign from positive in the 1950s

[7] Exhibition art is different. For example, painters sell unique pieces to individual consumers, and replication of the viewing experience is costly. The economics of such
transactions is consequently different.

[8] It is difficult to test such notions but, in addition to the Ravid (1999) study covered in
depth here, the reader may want to look at a nice empirical test of the star notion in the
music industry by Hamlen (1991).

to negative in the 1970s. The total number of awards received per film has a positive and significant effect on revenues.

Litman and Kohl (1989) find that the participation of stars and top directors, critical reviews, ratings, and several other variables are significantly related to revenues. However, Academy Award nominations are significant only for the best film category, and winning does not seem to affect revenues.

These studies, as well as some analyses of success in the business from other points of view (see Eliashberg and Shugan 1997; Eliashberg and Sawhney 1996), have focused on receipts. Chapter 4 offers many examples of this branch of the literature. In recent years, though, there have been several studies that have extended earlier work by adding variables and including return on investment. Ravid's (1999) study is based on a sample of close to 200 films in the early 1990s. It extended the literature in several ways, empirically and conceptually. Conceptually, it sought to explain the importance (or lack thereof) of stars to economic success, using the competing economic concepts of signaling (with an expensive star) as opposed to rent capture (stars capture all their value added).

Empirically, in addition to domestic theatrical revenues, which had been the focus of most previous research, and which currently represent less than 20 percent of the total receipts of a typical movie, Ravid (1999) includes video and international revenues. Indeed, it turns out that video revenues drive one of the most significant conclusions in the study.[9] Recently, many films have spawned merchandise and other products, which of course make films, and in particular animated films, even more valuable properties.[10] Therefore, the inclusion of additional sources provides

---

[9] *S&P Credit Week* (1997) reports that in 1996, video revenues were the largest component of the average film's revenues. This was not yet the case in Ravid's (1999) sample period (video revenues have grown about sevenfold between 1986 and 1996); still, the inclusion of video revenues and international theatrical revenues improves the accuracy of our revenue estimate compared to other recent studies.

[10] *The Lion King*, a very successful G-rated movie, cost $55 million to make in 1994. It took in $313 million in domestic theaters, $454 million abroad, and $520 million in video

a much better picture of where the money comes from in the industry. Second, Ravid uses a comprehensive set of control variables, including MPAA ratings,[11] sequel status, critical reviews, and release dates. The study also includes several alternative star definitions. Also, the study is based on a random sample, as opposed to top hundred or other non-neutral classifications, which were common in earlier work. Finally, Ravid also studies the return on investment rather than just revenues. This is important because most studies find that budgets are a main driver of revenues. Thus, it is easy to produce movies that gross a lot of money – just put in a lot of money. However, that may not be a profit-maximizing strategy.

In studying profitability, one is faced with many difficulties. First, although most movie studios are publicly traded companies, they do not have to report information on individual projects. Thus, much of the needed data is not public. Further, even if it were public, the nature of movie accounting (and other accounting, as shown by Enron, WorldCom, and others) is such that profit-and-loss statements must be pruned essentially line by line if one is to reach economically meaningful numbers. Thus, even if profit were reported, it would not necessarily be useful.[12] Ravid (1999) chooses a proxy measure: namely, total revenue over negative cost, which represents a good approximation for profit. This proxy does not include advertising and promotional costs, implicitly assuming that such costs are proportional to the budget.[13] Ravid finds that stars play no role in the financial success of a film. Univariate tests support the industry view that stars increase revenues. However, in multiple regressions,

revenues, but Disney also sold another $3 billion dollars worth of related merchandise (see Stevens and Grover 1998).

[11] Among all films rated, between 1968 and 2002, 58% were R-rated whereas only 7% were G-rated. In recent years, the percentage of G-rated films has decreased further and the percentage of R-rated films has increased (see MPAA website www.mpaa.org). This might have contributed to the findings reported here.

[12] Chapter 3 explores accounting in the industry in detail.

[13] Ravid and Basuroy (2004), who later collected these data for the same sample, found that the conjecture was right – in fact, the correlation is so high that it was difficult to run these cost components separately in a regression.

including budget figures, budgets seem to take much of the significance – in other words, big budget films may signal high revenues, regardless of the source of spending. Also, attention by reviewers seems to be important to success – the more reviews a film receives, the higher the revenues. Family-friendly ratings (G and PG) increase revenues as well, and sequels seem to do better. The latter point is consistent with the view that insiders are not better informed than outsiders but, when – for whatever elusive reason – a film succeeds, studios attempt to replicate the formula. Return regressions cannot reject the "rent capture" versus the signaling hypothesis. That is to say, stars' presence is not correlated with returns either. However, the role of budgets sees a dramatic reversal – big budgets do not contribute to profitability. If anything (as the final table in Ravid [1999] demonstrates), they may contribute to losses. Only G and PG ratings and reviewers' attention seem to matter (sequel status is marginally significant in some regressions). A later study on a completely different sample supports the view that budgets on average are bad for returns and, incidentally, also supports the important role of G and PG ratings in determining returns (see John, Ravid, and Sunder 2004).

Table 2.1 summarizes the results. For revenues, the important variables are budget, family ratings (G and PG), sequel status, and the number of critical reviews (index 4). The rate of return is significantly influenced only by G and PG ratings (G films' revenues include a very important video component) and, to some extent, by sequel status. Budget is insignificant. When one adds five very low-budget films included in the original sample, the budget variable becomes negative and significant. The findings in John, Ravid, and Sunder (2004) are similar but, due to the different construction of the sample, significance varies. Budgets affect rates of return in a negative and significant manner, and G and PG ratings are positive and significant.[14]

---

[14] John, Ravid, and Sunder (2004) focus on the role of directors in making successful films. The sample follows directors' careers and analyzes the rehiring decision (that is,

Table 2.1: *Revenues and the rate of return on movies*

| Variable | ln (Total Revenues) | Rate of Return |
|---|---|---|
| CONSTANT | −1.664 (−2.8) | −0.762 (−0.53) |
| LNBUDGET | 1.144 (10.62) | 0.137 (0.52) |
| AWARD | −0.114 (−0.45) | 0.192 (0.315) |
| UNKNOWN | 0.099 (0.43) | 0.0002 (0.00) |
| NEXT | 0.064 (0.22) | 0.100 (0.14) |
| G | 1.506 (2.49) | 4.52 (3.10) |
| PG | 1.295 (2.70) | 3.36 (2.90) |
| PG13 | 0.608 (1.31) | 1.02 (0.91) |
| R | 0.615 (1.38) | 1.06 (0.99) |
| INDEX1 | 0.369 (1.01) | 1.00 (1.13) |
| INDEX4 | 0.029 (2.63) | 0.03 (1.10) |
| RELEASE | 0.066 (0.13) | 0.132 (0.11) |
| SEQUEL | 0.828 (2.54) | 1.33 (1.69) |
| Adjusted $R^2$ | 0.675 | 0.165 |

The dependent variables are LNTOTREV, the log of total revenues, and the rate of return; i.e., revenues divided by the budget. Independent variables include dummy variables for ratings (G, PG, PG13, R – the default is nonrated films), dummies as to whether participants had received Academy Awards (AWARD), whether cast members could not be found in standard film references (UNKNOWN), and whether a cast member had participated in a top grossing film (NEXT). Additional variables include the log of the budget of the film (LNBUDGET), the number of reviews (INDEX4), the percentage of non-negative reviews (INDEX1), and a seasonality variable (RELEASE). Finally, we include a dummy for sequels (SEQUEL). *t*-statistics are reported between brackets under the coefficients. The number of observations is 175.
*Source:* Ravid (1999).

De Vany and Walls study the economics of the film industry from a somewhat different angle, focusing on the statistical distribution of film revenues. In general, they have much larger samples; however, they analyze only domestic theatrical revenues. Their conclusions, however, are very similar. De Vany and Walls (1999, 2002), for example, find that stars

choosing which directors direct again). They also find that rehiring is based on both financial and critical success and identify a significant ability component in directors' performance.

do not contribute to the profitability of films. The sample used in De Vany and Walls (2002) includes 2,015 films released between 1985 and 1996. They have more films than Ravid (1999), Ravid and Basuroy (2004), or John, Ravid, and Sunder (2004), but they collect less information on each individual movie. Their characterization of stars is different too. Their stars are people who appear in *Premier*'s annual list of the one hundred most powerful people in Hollywood.[15] De Vany and Walls (2002) find that the profit distribution of U.S. theatrical revenues is not symmetric. R-rated films are dominated in terms of revenues, returns on production costs, and profits (as defined by them).

Although the technical details are somewhat difficult, the point is simple: The distribution of returns is skewed – it is composed of many films that flop and some that are phenomenal hits rather than of many "average" films as a normal distribution would imply. Thus, one must worry about the predictive power of data analysis.[16] However, Table 5 in their study shows that only 6 percent of R-rated movies gross more than $50 million, whereas 13 percent of G- and PG-rated films succeed in doing so, as well as 10 percent of PG-13–rated films.

Similarly, 20 percent of G-rated films are hits (rates of return more than three times the production budget) as opposed to 16 percent for PG, 12 percent for PG-13, and only 11 percent for R-rated films. For G-rated films, the mean lies well to the right of the median. It is true also for other films, but less so. Thus, G-rated films stochastically dominate all other types almost everywhere.[17]

In a study that focuses on the choice of independent versus studio financing, Fee (2002) also runs a profit regression (using domestic

[15] Ravid (1999) uses several star definitions, including Academy Awards, nominations for awards, and participation in a top ten grossing film in the previous year.

[16] However, the distribution of total revenues is, in general, smoother than that of domestic revenues because films may make money in video, internationally, or in TV distribution, even if they do not do well domestically. This may make the profit distributions less skewed. For example, the finding that violent movies do well internationally will move the revenue distribution of R-rated films more to the center.

[17] Much of the work mentioned here and in other essays is included in De Vany (2004).

box-office data and budgets) on his sample of 349 films from 1992 to 1993. He finds that G-rated films perform the best. Simonoff and Sparrow (2000) use a different sample: films released in 1997–98. Only domestic revenues are considered. However, the G-factor seems to be there, despite the fact that the main source of income of G-rated films is video revenues (not included in their sample) and that international revenues matter.

To summarize the conclusions of these recent profitability studies, big-budget movies lead to higher revenues but generally to somewhat lower rates of return. Stars do not help or hurt movies. What seems to be important for return on investment is a G or PG rating and, to some extent, sequel status.

This summary leaves us with three major puzzles. First, if indeed stars do not contribute to profitability, why hire them?[18] Does the industry simply not know what is going on? Are they unaware of all the studies or are they just ignoring them?[19]

Second, if the consistent finding that G-rated films perform better is correct, why is it that so few G-rated films are being produced? The puzzle becomes even more pronounced after noting that the huge success of G-rated films is not a new or surprising phenomenon – the past is all about G-rated films. Ravid (1999) compiles the list of top ten films of all times (adjusted for inflation). It is dominated by G-rated films, including the likes of *Bambi* and *Fantasia*. However, the percentage of R-rated films produced, which has always been (too?) high, has not declined but has increased over the years, including the recent past. So, is indeed

[18] There were academic studies in other areas attempting to test the star phenomenon, following Rosen (1981) and the other superstar papers. However, data problems and elusive proxy definitions have made empirical studies difficult. For an interesting attempt, see Hamlen (1991).

[19] This latter possibility is probably not true. Ravid (1999) was cited in *Variety* several times, as well as in the *Hollywood Reporter*, the *New York Times*, the *Wall Street Journal* as late as December 2003, and in media around the world. The study was also requested by dozens of industry executives. Much attention was awarded to studies by De Vany and Walls as well.

Hollywood producing too many R-rated movies, as De Vany and Walls (2002) ask and, if so, why?[20]

The third puzzle is Hollywood's pursuit of so-called "event movies" (*Pearl Harbor* and *Spiderman* are recent examples) which, by definition, are expensive action-packed films. If big budgets are not good for you, why not just go for a slate of small films instead?

Some new work by Ravid and Basuroy (2004) and Basuroy, Chatterjee, and Ravid (2003) shows that all three puzzles can be interpreted as seemingly suboptimal risk-management strategies by extremely risk-averse executives.[21] There may be evidence also for revenue or sales maximization.[22] In other words, if executives care much more about avoiding failures than about big hits, their observed choices are more easily explained. In particular, parceling the R-rated movies into categories reveals that some categories, in particular very violent movies, increase revenues and lower risk, even though they do not contribute to profitability. Ravid and Basuroy (2004) show that the returns on very violent films tend to cluster around the mean. About 71 percent of the very violent films are in the 6th through 9th deciles of returns, whereas only 23 percent of these movies are in the lowest four deciles. For films that contain both sex and violence, the picture is similar but somewhat less appealing – 71 percent of these films are in the 5th through 9th deciles. No film of this category is in the lowest decile, whereas the percentage for the bottom four is 29 percent. However, no film that is very violent or that features sex and violence is in the uppermost decile of returns either (see Table 2.2).

---

[20] The tide may be turning in the twenty-first century as studios bow to overwhelming economic evidence. Several *Variety* articles in 2002 described a turn towards more family production; for example, see Bing (2002).

[21] There are several papers that demonstrate such effects in other industries, including Tufano (1996), Chevalier and Ellison (1997), and Haushalter (2000). The literature on these issues can be traced back to Baumol (1958), Williamson (1964), and Holmstrom (1979). Important later theoretical studies include Smith and Stulz (1985); Froot, Scharfstein, and Stein (1992); and DeMarzo and Duffie (1995). See also Jin (2002) and Lim and Wang (2003).

[22] For a discussion of these concepts, see Fershtman and Judd (1987) and Zabojnic (1998).

Table 2.2a: *The percentages of different types of films in various ROI deciles.*

| ROI Deciles | ROI Range | VV[a] | SEXV | Violent | Sequels |
|---|---|---|---|---|---|
| 10th Decile | 5.79–17.05 | 0 | 0 | 0.04 | 0.27 |
| 9th Decile | 3.53–5.74 | 0.18 | 0.29 | 0.15 | 0.27 |
| 8th Decile | 2.56–3.52 | 0.06 | 0.12 | 0.13 | 0.18 |
| 7th Decile | 1.89–2.33 | 0.35 | 0.06 | 0.17 | 0.18 |
| 6th Decile | 1.30–1.85 | 0.12 | 0.12 | 0.06 | 0.09 |
| 5th Decile | 1.00–1.29 | 0.06 | 0.12 | 0.11 | 0 |
| 4th Decile | 0.70–0.98 | 0 | 0.06 | 0.13 | 0 |
| 3rd Decile | 0.50–0.69 | 0.12 | 0.18 | 0.09 | 0 |
| 2nd Decile | 0.34–0.49 | 0 | 0.06 | 0.04 | 0 |
| 1st Decile | 0.09–0.29 | 0.12 | 0 | 0.09 | 0 |

This table shows the rates of return from various types of films, divided into deciles. Violent films are R-rated films that are described as violent by the MPAA. Very Violent (VV) films are films that are described as violent with a qualifying adjective such as extremely violent or graphic violence. SEXV are films that are rated both for violence and for sexual or sensual content.

*Source:* Ravid and Basuroy (2003).

In other words, returns on very violent films are not stellar, but they are more predictable than average. Basuroy and Ravid (2004) further calculate that among the 175 films in the sample, 59.4 percent have a rate of return that is greater than one (see Table 2.2b). This percentage is lower for all R-rated films, where only 56.4 percent "break even," consistent with all previous work. Violent films as a whole break even less often than other films. On the other hand, fully 77 percent of the very violent films, as well as 71 percent of the films with sex and violence, "break even."[23] Thus, producing violent films may not be a profit-maximizing strategy, but it is a safer bet for executives.

Basuroy et al. (2003) present some additional evidence that, to some extent, explains the star and event-movies puzzles. Basuroy et al. (2003)

---

[23] I put "break even" in quotes, because the measure is revenues over budget. Not all revenues accrue to the producing studios, and the budget is augmented by advertising expenses. Therefore, movies that "break even" here actually lose money for the studio. However, results are not very sensitive to the choice of the break-even point (see De Vany and Walls 1997).

Table 2.2b: *Proportion of films that "Break Even."*

| | Proportion of other R-rated films | Proportion of all other films | Z-value when compared with other R-rated films | Z-value when compared with all other films |
|---|---|---|---|---|
| SEX (0.58) | 0.554 | 0.599 | 0.28 | 0.22 |
| SEXV (0.705) | 0.532 | 0.582 | 1.33* | 1.01 |
| VV (0.765) | 0.519 | 0.578 | 1.81** | 1.36*** |
| V (0.383) | 0.745 | 0.672 | −3.56*** | −2.49*** |
| SEQUEL (0.909) | N/A | 0.573 | N/A | 2.20* |

*** Significant at 0.01 level; ** significant at 0.05 level; * significant at 0.10 level. This table shows the proportion of films that break even in various categories. "Break even" is defined as total revenues/budget >1, which is not the same as being profitable. *Source:* Ravid and Basuroy (2003).

separate their sample of about two hundred movies into movies that received mostly positive reviews and movies that received mostly negative reviews. They find that big budgets and stars contribute more to profitability in movies that are panned by critics, whereas they contribute nothing (statistically) to the success of films that are praised by critics. Thus, it may be that event movies and stars provide some "insurance" against a bad product. In other words, if a studio is not convinced about the reception its movie will enjoy, then a big star and expensive special effects may soften the blow should a blow occur. Such strategies are not optimal if one seeks to increase the expected rate of return, as shareholders would like, but they make sense in an environment where an executive who greenlights an expensive flop may be summarily kicked out.

There is further evidence of seemingly suboptimal hedging on the part of movie executives. Einav (2003) discusses seasonality in film attendance. He separates attendance numbers into two parts: seasonal patterns in underlying demand, and changes in observed attendance as a result of specific movie releases. His empirical analysis shows that seasonal patterns are much flatter than industry seems to think and, thus, movies seem to be wrongly clustered during peak holiday periods. Why is that? Einav suggests that distributors are likely to be conservative rather than risk their jobs, reputation, and potentially future business because of a movie failure that would be attributed to a poor release decision. This is fully consistent with the conservatism and risk aversion documented in the other work cited herein. More generally, allowing for suboptimal risk-minimizing strategies on the part of executives can at least partially explain some seemingly puzzling decisions in the movie business.

## CONTRACTS

Contracts define incentives, thus enabling us to further study and understand the decisions, which lead to production and ultimately profitability. I focus on contracts within the production process: namely, between talent and producers. There are, of course, interesting issues also regarding exhibition contracts, and contracts for buying or optioning property – for instance, studios may option screenplays for a given period of time and then rights revert to the writer. Discussion of contracts between distributors and exhibitors, however, is deferred to Chapter 5.

During the studio era, contracts for artists, including directors and actors, essentially gave studios options on their employment for seven years. For their part, studios could renegotiate or terminate the contract every six or twelve months. Actors essentially could not quit. Also, they had little control over the roles they played. Clearly, star players had more favorable renegotiation terms and input, and studios varied in how they exercised their option (Caves 2000). However, in general, studios were able to reap the rents should a star emerge.

The studio system was dismantled by the Paramount decision (1948), which prohibited vertical integration, and by the emergence of TV, which created a natural market for movies that did not have a wide theatrical appeal. According to Caves (2000), the high tax rates during World War II were an additional factor, encouraging stars and other highly paid talent to form corporations rather than be employees. The combination of these factors gradually created the project-by-project system that exists today.

The project-by-project system now dominates the industry. Contracts between talent and producers or studios provide either fixed fees, or fixed fees and a participation share, either from gross receipts or from net receipts. Participation contracts are now the norm, but one can trace their emergence to the studio era. Chapter 3 offers the details of such contracts, but I take a broader viewpoint. Weinstein (1998) traces the first net-profit contract to the agreement between playwright David Belasco and Warner Brothers for *Tiger Rose* in 1923. Although the definition of net differs from current practice, the structure of the contract was comparable to contemporary net-profit contracts.

Similarly, as early as 1930, Al Jolson had a gross-participation contract and so did John Barrymore (the latter contract was from the first dollar). In 1939, James Cagney received a contract covering eleven movies for $150,000 per film plus 10 percent of the gross over $1.5 million. Weinstein (1998) suggests that the financially stronger studios (such as MGM) rarely used participation contracts, whereas the weaker ones such as Warner, RKO, and Universal found them attractive. This implies that both a cash constraint and risk-sharing motive may drive the use of share contracts. The latter motive seems more persuasive when one considers that only (presumably rich) major stars received profit-sharing contracts. Share contracts became more pervasive as studios started financing and distributing independent productions in the 1950s and are now the norm.

Weinstein discusses the incentive structure of participation contracts, using the following conceptual framework. Denote the gross receipts by G, and the budget by C. A gross-participation contract will specify a share $\alpha \times G$ for talent, but a net-participation contract will specify a different sharing rule, $\beta \, (G - C)$, where $\alpha$ and $\beta$ are fractions. Weinstein (1998) argues that the computation of net profit is, in fact, in the interest of the talent because it prespecifies what costs will, in fact, be deducted from gross revenues. However, there is still leeway for studio manipulation.

Further, as this very simple formulation suggests, net-profit contracts create an incentive for studios to inflate costs because the talent shares in these costs.

It is perhaps these incentives that contribute to the very bad reputation of net-profit contracts in the industry. If incentives are ignored, net-profit contracts can be simply viewed as similar to out-of-the-money stock-option contracts. An excellent series of articles in *Hollywood Reporter* (1991) by David Robb shows how net-profit contracts are used and abused. The articles establish a tendency to inflate costs and show that net profits were indeed unlikely to be realized, using very nice case studies. For example, the movie *Who Framed Roger Rabbit?*, which cost a little more than $50 million to produce, had revenues in excess of $205 million by December 31, 1990. Yet, the profit statement sent to investors showed a loss of close to $20 million. This does sound outrageous, except the fact that agreed-upon fees and interest added up to more than $90 million, whereas advertising and publicity costs reached almost another $50 million, in addition to miscellaneous other expense items.[24]

Why use profit-sharing contracts at all? There are several possible justifications – a few are of a general nature and others may be specific to the movie industry.[25]

> *Agency problems:* The most obvious conjecture is that such contracts may solve agency problems. In other words, contracts can be used for incentives, to make sure that a participant works hard, similar to a CEO's compensation contracts. It is unlikely, however, that this is the motivation in the motion picture industry. Because of the "free agent" status and the project-by-project nature of the industry, a failure will have dire long-term consequences for an

[24] One should also note that revenues are shared approximately equally between studios (who receive what are termed rentals) and exhibitors; thus, before one starts being outraged, revenues must be halved.

[25] The following analysis corresponds closely with Weinstein (1998) and Chisholm (1997).

actor or director (see John, Ravid, and Sunder 2004). Given this reality, little additional incentive seems necessary.

*Risk sharing:* Weinstein shows that the coefficient of variation of movie revenues (standard deviation/mean) has increased over time. Also, the concentration ratio of revenues has increased – whereas the top 1 percent of films represented 2–3 percent of revenues in the 1940s, this had increased to more than 10 percent by 1993. Thus, risks have increased. In the standard setting, if the star is risk-averse relative to the studio, a participation contract should be more expensive for the studio than a fixed-fee contract and should thus be avoided. However, one can make the opposite argument regarding relative risk preferences as well. Perhaps stars are more diversified (they work on many projects) and richer, whereas a studio may be heavily committed to a single project, with decisions made by individuals who are risk-averse and afraid of being fired, as I argued in the previous section. Thus, profit-sharing contracts can share risks as well.

*Asymmetric information:* It may be that the willingness to accept participation contracts suggests that stars or directors know more about the prospects of the film in question and, thus, value shares in the project more highly than the studio does. A casual example is *Forrest Gump,* for which Tom Hanks and Bob Zemeckis received no salary but rather a percentage of the gross receipts. James Cameron in *Titanic* had a similar deal. Ravid (1999) provides weak evidence in support of this idea – in small-budget films (under $20 million) with stars, star indicators seem to be somewhat correlated with returns.

*Contracting costs:* Finally, it may be that studios would like to save on contracting costs. Participation contracts effectively defer payments of large amounts of money. Consequently, the upfront budget is lower and it may be easier for the studio to raise money for the project. Naturally, investors will receive less money later on, but if there are capital constraints, this type of argument may hold water.

Chisholm (1997) studies 118 talent contracts over thirty years. Only forty-nine of these contracts involved share payments. She finds that actors are likely to receive share contracts for projects that have a longer production time. This finding can be interpreted various ways, but it can support the notion that share contracts are more likely if a less transparent project is at stake and if monitoring is more difficult for a complex, lengthy project.

There is positive correlation between the probability of receiving a share contract and between revenues from previous movies. The incidence of such contracts also increases with experience – successful and more experienced actors may need greater incentives than people who are just starting out.[26] The "previous work as a team" variable and the trend variable have positive coefficients, the latter meaning that the probability of receiving these contracts has been increasing through time. Also, actresses are less likely to receive share contracts. Measures of risk (the financial status of the studio) and liquidity issues (the real budget) were added, but the results were mixed. On the other hand, the sample is relatively small, and the measures can be debated.

Finally, Chisholm uses a more elaborate procedure to estimate the determinants of the fixed payment where available. First, she calculates the selection criterion, and only then tests whether star characteristics determine the amount of fixed payments for the contracts where such data is available. The same variables remain significant, except that variables such as "Oscar" or "experience" lose significance. According to Chisholm, this is evidence that star characteristics determine whether a share contract is offered but not the size of the payment.

Weinstein claims that Chisholm's results are consistent with risk sharing (the star is richer and more experienced) and liquidity constraints (the total expected compensation, not included in the study as a variable,

---

[26] This is consistent with arguments and findings in, for example, Gibbons and Murphy (1992).

increases with experience and success of recent films). However, there is certainly an incentive interpretation for these results – experience and Oscars establish a track record and, thus, an actor may decide not to make an effort in a particular movie because one failure will not count that much against him.

John, Ravid, and Sunder (2004) study another aspect of the elaborate process that defines the creation of a movie: namely, the evolution of directors' careers. The questions they address are whether the best directors indeed "survive" in this new world of contracting and whether the project-by-project environment is a result of an incentive structure or is the outcome of a learning (or ability-revelation) process. Their empirical results support the ability revelation and risk-sharing interpretation rather than the incentive effect.

Their study shows that a large percentage of directors direct one theatrical movie and drop out. This very quick updating as to the qualifications for this not-very-well-defined job is supported by DeVany (2002), who looks at several thousand movies. In his sample, the probability of directing a second film given that you have directed one film is only 35 percent. However, after you have directed five films, the probability increases to 76 percent, and it reaches 90 percent at fifteen films (see ibid., Table 2).

John, Ravid, and Sunder (2004) further analyze how directors are hired. They find that directors are more likely to be hired if they have a good track record, both in terms of profitability and in terms of critical reviews. The significant-critical-reviews variable reflects the latest movie, whereas for profits, the decision rests on the average of all past projects. This means that common industry wisdom, which suggests that "you are as good as your last movie," may not be correct and people are judged on their entire career path, as they should be.

Further, John, Ravid, and Sunder (2004) find a director-fixed-effect on profitability. In other words, after accounting for all variables that were found to matter in previous research, there is still a profit contribution that can be attributable to the director. John, Ravid, and Sunder find that directors who survive in the profession provide positive added value to the films they direct. Further, these fixed-effects coefficients are positively correlated with the number of films made by the director. This fits the idea of a gradual learning process, in which, as more information accumulates, the directors with lesser ability are weeded out and only the best remain. Of our seventy directors for which all data is available, twenty-six have positive and significant fixed effects; only four directors have negative and significant fixed effects.

There are quite a few other interesting aspects of contracting in the production process that have not yet been discussed. For instance, stars often have pay-or-play contracts. These contracts essentially commit the star's time in advance to the project; however, should the project be scrapped, the star will get paid anyway. Viewed in this light, some decisions to go ahead with questionable projects may look quite a bit more reasonable. At the point in time where the extent of the disaster begins to be clear, much of the cost is sunk and, therefore, going ahead may be a profit-maximizing decision.

Similarly, star contracts are replete with perks, some of which may seem excessive. In one contract I examined, the star requested a specific hotel suite, several first-class tickets at the studio's expense for his friends to travel to the filming location, and a job tailored specifically to one of his friends, which paid rather handsomely.

This may look like one of these excess stories associated with Hollywood. However, when star salaries are more than $20 million for about ten weeks of work, any concession by the star, such as agreeing to extend the contractual length of principal photography to eleven weeks, may more than compensate the studio for any perks the star may require.[27]

---

[27] It actually gets better. Consider the example I began in the text. If filming were indeed to take eleven weeks and the star had agreed to a ten-week schedule, the eleventh week would have added $2 million to his or her salary. Any additional week would cost another $2 million. However, if he or she agreed to eleven weeks, then the eleventh week would, of course, cost nothing more, and each additional week would be priced at 20/11; i.e., $1.82 million.

A contract theoretic look at such issues, which may be interesting as an application of agency theory, is hindered by the fact that it is virtually impossible to assemble a large sample of talent contracts that are all privately signed and rarely made available to outsiders. Hopefully, some studio or organization, however, will indeed enable researchers to consider these problems for the benefit of science and the studios themselves.

In the final section, I would like to move from the present to the future and speculate as to how the digital (r)evolution will affect the production process.

## THE DIGITAL (R)EVOLUTION

Whereas in the previous sections I discussed findings of work based on past history, this section is my projection for the future of production, which is based on study and history but no solid, scientific evidence. It looks very likely, however, that digitalization will dramatically change the face of film production distribution and exhibition. The changes are beginning to be felt already. Chapter 5 discusses how digitalization is affecting theatrical exhibition (both through digital projection and through piracy), and I focus on the digitalization of production, with inevitable mention of other issues. A flurry of copyright suits on the one hand and the phenomenal success of digitally created films, such as the recent *Finding Nemo, Shrek,* and others, reflect the two very different ways in which digitalization is changing the economics of media and entertainment. The media and the legal profession have focused on piracy and illegal copying. However, the revolution is perhaps somewhere else.

Digitalization has made copying of music and films easier and cheaper. However, this is not the first, second, or even third time that easier reproduction of intellectual property has forced an introduction of a changed legal and business model. Perhaps the first major legal action against ease of copying ended up in the Supreme Court almost a century ago. In

1908, Adam Geibel, the composer of "Little Cotton Dolly" and "Kentucky Babe," and White-Smith, the company that published his music sheets, sued, regarding unauthorized mechanical reproduction of his music in the so-called player pianos (pianolas) made by Apollo. Replacing the word mechanical with the word electronic makes this sound eerily contemporary. The Supreme Court upheld lower-court rulings against the composer and the publisher (*White-Smith v. Apollo*, 209 U.S. 1, 1908) and allowed Apollo to reproduce the music without paying this composer. However, that was not the end of the story. Laws were changed in 1909 to provide copyright protection for the new medium.

Later on, musicians sued phonograph makers, and legal actions were brought against radio, by studios against TV (which made movies available for free to wide audiences . . . sound familiar?), and, finally, by studios against producers of videocassettes. In each case, after prolonged legal wrangling, a new legal framework and a new pricing model emerged, enabling both sides to share in the profits. Today, income from TV, video, and DVDs exceeds U.S. theatrical revenues for the average movie. So far, then, movie and music copyright battles have had a reasonably happy ending, which seems to imply that people do prefer to do things legitimately. Society just needs a pricing scheme reflecting a new cost structure. Today, a new scheme is already starting to emerge, with the introduction of legal music and movie downloading services. However, the process is still in the making. Keep in mind that in 1998, only six years ago, Shawn Fanning was still studying programming, and now Napster is an important piece of digital history.

Perhaps the more revolutionary, rather than evolutionary, change brought about by digitalization is at the other end of the production cycle. Although multimillion-dollar movies still dominate the headlines, independents are now able to produce technically more accomplished films for less money than ever before. Digital cameras enable the independent film maker to repeat shots without budget constraints. Lighting, which is costly and complicated, is less of an issue in the digitally alterable film, and shots can be viewed in real time. In the foreseeable future, digital transmission and projection will enable independent film makers to cost-lessly distribute their goods, just like the big guys.

This, however, is just the beginning. Today, even run-of-the-mill comedies or dramas require four-hundred computer-generated shots on average, and in industry circles some jokes suggested that the World War II epic *Pearl Harbor* should have competed for the animated Academy Award, given the number of computer-generated special effects in the movie.

One day, a writer with the right software will be able to create a theatrical quality movie, animate actors or other digitally created images, and costlessly and instantaneously deliver the finished product to theaters and to home projection devices around the world. Technologically, this is already possible, but the quality is still not quite there and the complexity of the process is prohibitive. Once the final technological and economic hurdles have been overcome, the digitalization of the film-making process should have two effects, both leading to democratization of the art of movie making. First and foremost, creating movies will become similar to writing books. Second, movies that are of interest to very limited audiences will become financially viable.

This brave new future puts the cumbersome machinery of a conven-tional studio at a disadvantage. However, before eulogizing entertainment companies as they exist today, one should remember that everybody can write books or paint portraits right now, but very few writers or painters sell well. In other words, even if authors are able to create movies al-most single-handedly, they may still need marketing muscle to sell. In the first half of the twentieth century, studios saw themselves mainly as production companies. As the century ended, their major role involved financing. However, as digitalization evolves in the twenty-first century, they may end up as marketing and distribution entities for authors, just like book-publishing companies.

## CONCLUSION

This chapter surveyed some of the economic research regarding film production. Despite the industry's view that "nobody knows anything," there are systematic patterns in the success of movies, as well as systematic biases in the decision processes that can be explained as risk-averse behavior by executives in charge. In particular, most studies seem to show that family movies do better, whereas there is little evidence to show that stars provide many long-term economic benefits.

I argued that, despite these findings, studios tend to produce too many R-rated films and use too many special effects and stars. Much of this seemingly puzzling behavior can be explained by allowing for extreme failure aversion. I then described the contracts between talent and management and surveyed research into the form these contracts take. Perhaps the most interesting phenomenon I considered was the prevalence of participation contracts. The surveyed literature seems to indicate that such contracts are awarded optimally for incentive, asymmetric information, or risk-sharing reasons. Finally, the chapter offers some ideas and projections regarding the future of production in the digital age, arguing that in the twenty-first century, film production will become more democratic – more people will be able to produce more films suited for increasingly segmented audiences.

### REFERENCES

Adler, Moshe. 1985. "Stardom and Talent," *American Economic Review*, 75: 208–12.

Barker, Robert. 2003. "Watch the Movie, Skip the IPO," *BusinessWeek*, December 15.

Basuroy, Suman, Subimal Chatterjee, and S. Abraham Ravid. 2003. "How Critical Are Critical Reviews? The Box Office Effects of Film Critics, Star Power, and Budgets," *Journal of Marketing*, 67(4).

Baumol, William. 1958. "On the Theory of Oligopoly," *Economica*, 25: 187–98.

Bing, Jonathan. 2002. "Hollywood Hot to Trot with Tots," *Variety*, April 29.

Caves, Richard E. 2000. *Creative Industries: Contracts between Art and Commerce*, Cambridge, MA: Harvard University Press.

Chevalier, Judith, and Glenn Ellison. 1997. "Risk Taking by Mutual Funds as a Response to Incentives," *Journal of Political Economy*, 105: 1167–1200.

Chisholm, Darlene C. 1997. "Profit Sharing vs. Fixed Payment Contracts – Evidence from the Motion Picture Industry," *Journal of Law, Economics and Organization*, 13(1): 169–201.

DeMarzo, Peter M., and Darrell Duffie. 1995. "Corporate Incentives for Hedging and Hedge Accounting," *Review of Financial Studies*, 8: 743–71.

De Vany, Arthur. 2004. *Hollywood Economics: How Extreme Uncertainty Shapes the Film Industry*, New York: Routledge.

De Vany, Arthur, and W. David Walls. 1997. "The Market for Motion Pictures: Rank, Revenue and Survival," *Economic Inquiry*, 35: 783–97.

———. 1999. "Uncertainty in the Movie Industry: Does Star Power Reduce the Terror at the Box Office?" *Journal of Cultural Economics*, 23: 285–318.

———. 2002. "Does Hollywood Make Too Many R-Rated Movies? Risk, Stochastic Dominance, and the Illusion of Expectation," *Journal of Business*, 75: 425–51.

Einav, Liran. 2003. "Gross Seasonality and Underlying Seasonality: Evidence from the U.S. Motion Picture Industry," unpublished manuscript, Economics Department, Stanford University.

Eliashberg, Jehoshua, and Mohanbir S. Sawhney. 1996. "A Parsimonious Model for Forecasting Gross Box-Office Revenues of Motion Pictures," *Marketing Science*, 15: 113–31.

Eliashberg, Jehoshua, and Steven M. Shugan. 1997. "Film Critics: Influencers or Predictors?" *Journal of Marketing*, 61: 68–78.

Fee, C. Edward. 2002. "The Costs of Outside Equity Control: Evidence from Motion Picture Financing Decisions," *Journal of Business*, 75: 681–711.

Fershtman, Chaim, and Kenneth L. Judd. 1987. "Equilibrium Incentives in Oligopoly," *American Economic Review*, 77: 927–40.

Froot, Kenneth, David Scharfstein, and Jeremy Stein. 1992. "Herd on the Street: Information Inefficiencies in the Market with Short-Term Speculation," *Journal of Finance*, 47: 1461–84.

Gibbons, Robert, and Kevin J. Murphy. 1992. "Optimal Incentive Contracts in the Presence of Career Concerns: Theory and Evidence," *Journal of Political Economy*, 100(3): 468–505.

Goettler, Ronald, and Phillip Leslie. 2003. "Co-financing to Manage Risk in the Motion Picture Industry," unpublished manuscript, Tepper School of Business, Carnegie Mellon University.

Hamlen, William A. 1991. "Superstardom in Popular Music: Empirical Evidence," *Review of Economics and Statistics*, 73: 729–33.

Haushalter, G. David. 2000. "Financing Policy, Basis Risk and Corporate Hedging: Evidence from Oil and Gas Producers," *Journal of Finance*, 55: 107–52.

Holmstrom, Bengt. 1979. "Moral Hazard and Observability," *Bell Journal of Economics*, 10: 74–91.

Jensen, Michael C., and William H. Meckling. 1976. "Theory of the Firm: Managerial Behavior, Agency Costs and Ownership Structure," *Journal of Financial Economics*, 3: 305–60.

Jin, Li. 2002. "CEO Compensation, Diversification and Incentives," *Journal of Financial Economics*, 66(1): 29–63.

John, Kose, S. Abraham Ravid, and Jayanthi Sunder. 2004. "Performance and Managerial Turnover: Evidence from the Career Paths of Film Directors," unpublished manuscript, New York University Stern School of Business.

Landers, Peter, and Joann S. Lublin. 2003. "Merck's Big Bet on Research by Its Scientists Comes up Short," *Wall Street Journal*, November 28.

Lim, Sonya S., and Heli C. Wang. 2003. "The Effect of Financial Hedging on the Incentives for Corporate Diversification: The Role of Stakeholder Firm-Specific Investments," unpublished manuscript, Finance Department, DePaul University.

Litman, Barry R. 1983. "Predicting the Success of Theatrical Movies: An Empirical Study," *Journal of Popular Culture*, 17: 159–75.

Litman, Barry R. 1998. *The Motion Picture Mega-Industry*, Needham Heights, MA: Allyn and Bacon.

Litman, Barry R., and Linda S. Kohl. 1989. "Predicting Financial Success of Motion Pictures: The 80's Experience," *Journal of Media Economics*, 2: 35–49.

MacDonald, Glenn M. 1988. "The Economics of Rising Stars," *American Economic Review*, 78: 155–67.

Palia, Darius, S. Abraham Ravid, and Natalia Reisel. 2004. "Choosing to Co-Finance: An Analysis of Project-Specific Alliances in the Film Industry," unpublished manuscript, Rutgers University.

Ravid, S. Abraham. 1999. "Information, Blockbusters and Stars," *Journal of Business*, 72: 463–92.

Ravid, S. Abraham. 2004. "Are They All Crazy, or Just Risk Averse? Some Movie Puzzles and Possible Solutions," in *The Economics of Art and Culture*, Victor Ginsbeurgh (ed.), Amsterdam: Elsevier.

Ravid, S. Abraham, and Suman Basuroy. 2004. "Executive Objective Function, the R-Rating Puzzle and the Production of Violent Movies," *Journal of Business*, 77(2).

Robb, David. 1991. *Hollywood Reporter.*

Rosen, Sherwin. 1981. "The Economics of Superstars," *American Economic Review*, 71: 845–58.

Simonoff, Jeffrey, and Ilana R. Sparrow. 2000. "Predicting Movie Grosses: Winners and Losers, Blockbusters and Sleepers," *Chance*, 13: 15–24.

Smith, Sharon P., and V. Kerry Smith. 1986. "Successful Movies: A Preliminary Empirical Analysis," *Applied Economics*, 18: 501–7.

Smith, Clifford W., and René M. Stulz. 1985. "The Determinants of Firms Hedging Policies," *Journal of Financial and Quantitative Analysis*, 20: 391–405.

*S&P Credit Week.* 1997. "Are the cameras ready to roll on securitizing the movies?" September 3.

Stevens, Elizabeth L., and Ronald Grover. 1998. "The Entertainment Glut," *BusinessWeek*, February 16.

Tufano, Peter. 1996. "Who Manages Risk? An Empirical Examination of Risk Management Practices in the Gold-Mining Industry," *Journal of Finance* 31: 1097–1137.

Weinstein, Mark. 1998. "Profit-Sharing Contracts in Hollywood: Evolution and Analysis," *Journal of Legal Studies*, 27: 67–112.

Vogel, Harold L. 2001. *Entertainment Industry Economics: A Guide for Financial Analysis*, 5th ed. New York: Cambridge University Press.

Williamson, Oliver E. 1964. *The Economics of Discretionary Behavior: Managerial Objectives and the Theory of the Firm*, Englewood Cliffs, NJ: Prentice Hall.

Zabojnik, Jan. 1998. "Sales Maximization and Specific Human Capital," *RAND Journal of Economics*, 29: 790–802.

**3**

# Movie Industry Accounting[1]

### HAROLD L. VOGEL

Juxtapose the words "movie" and "accounting" and you have fodder for late-night television comedy or raging complaints by Hollywood heavyweights or visions of Frankenstein kitchens in which different sets of books are cooked. Even without cooking, the books themselves are often regarded as works of fiction. This chapter attempts to show why such views are, for the most part, largely exaggerated, untrue, or based on ignorance and misinformation.

## THEORY AND PRACTICE

Accounting systems are designed to enable owners and potential investors to realistically portray the health and viability of any project or business. In the case of movies and television, the prospective investor may be a trader of the company's shares as well as an actor, producer, director, or some other type of financial participant. Although financial reports must be tailored specifically for the needs of the different participants,

---

[1] This article informally accompanies the analysis presented in Chapter 4 of my text, *Entertainment Industry Economics: A Guide for Financial Analysis*, 6th ed., Cambridge University Press, 2004.

the reports are all derived from the same project sources and are based on commonly accepted rules and definitions for recognition of revenues, expenses, and, hopefully, profits.

Investors and traders in the shares of large companies, for instance, do not need nor necessarily want to know how every participant in every film distributed or produced by the company has been compensated. Conversely, creative participants will typically be more interested in the compensation potential from their own film projects than in how the global conglomerate that owns the studio also managed to profit and grow from investments in cable networks and systems, broadcast stations, recorded music operations, theme parks, and myriad other ventures.

As such, it's different strokes for different folks. Like the photograph of an object taken from different angles, viewing the same thing from another position reveals a different facet. That doesn't make the accounting inherently mysterious, nefarious, underhanded, or crooked. When abuses occasionally occur, it's the dishonest people, not the system, that are usually at fault.

The overall methods of accounting for business activities are governed by what are known as Generally Accepted Accounting Principles (GAAP). These differ from country to country, although the gaps among different country GAAPs are gradually being narrowed over time via statements issued by the International Accounting Standards committees. As technology advances and new industries develop or older ones evolve, continuous refinements and changes in already existing accounting treatments are required.

Among the major issues that are invariably of concern to accountants attempting to adjust and update GAAP are timing and event rules for recognition of revenue and expense items and for treatments of things like depreciation schedules, stock options, and taxes. Changes in the treatments of such items are fiercely and frequently debated by accounting and industry professionals through exposure drafts.[2] These exposure drafts are then voted on and eventually issued in the United States as published rulings by the Financial Accounting Standards Board (FASB). The revenue and expense recognition issues that are a standard feature of movie-accounting disputes are thus simply a microcosm of theoretical debates that appear in the larger context of setting overall corporate or partnership entity accounting policies.

All businesses, furthermore, face theoretical and practical issues in terms of cash versus accrual accounting and shareholder versus tax bookkeeping (which uses fully legal and allowable but different depreciation schedules than those seen in reports to shareholders). Cash accounting would work relatively well if everyone settled out obligations at precisely the same time. But, in most businesses, movies included, the expenses are paid out at one point in time and the revenues come in at another. A film producer must, for example, first pay cash out of pocket for salaries, catering trucks, sets, lodging and travel, insurance, electricity, and probably another thousand categories before a single penny of income is returned. Even after the revenue starts to be generated, it may be insufficient to cover total costs. And even if it is sufficient, revenue arrives at different times and at different rates from different sources, sometimes as cash, sometimes as credits. The diverse sources might include theatrical box-office receipts or sales of cable rights, broadcast rights, DVDs, T-shirts, or toys.

Expense and revenue streams are thus always unevenly disbursed and received over time, and there will inevitably be many theoretically defensible bookkeeping methods with which to account for these streams. To stay alive, though, businesses must operate ethically and legally or else lose the trust and confidence of their industry counterparts, clients,

---

[2] Exposure drafts are preliminary versions of proposed changes to rules. They are made public, and comments and suggestions are encouraged for a limited amount of time.

and customers. These aspects are especially important in the relatively small and intimate relationships that are commonly needed for the highly collaborative art form of filmmaking.

Although accounting theory in relation to economic, financial, and legal concepts and principles is broadly relevant to any type of accounting discussion, the main theoretical and philosophical issues encompass a large separate field of research, with little specificity to movie and entertainment production and distribution activities. For those who wish to delve deeper into the conceptual framework of accounting, papers by Watts and Zimmerman (1990) and Dopuch and Sunder (1980) are a good place to begin. As Watts and Zimmerman note in their summary (p. 152),

> Accounting numbers are used in different ways across industries. Besides the obvious regulatory uses of accounting numbers in financial institutions and public utilities, differences in industries' opportunity sets are likely to affect the accepted set of accounting methods.

As shall be seen, the more we learn about movie accounting, the more we can appreciate this point of view.

### HISTORICAL SETTING

The 1950s and early 1960s witnessed several structural changes in the relationship between corporations and creative participants. The changes included the end of the studio system, in which stars were kept under long-term contracts over many years, the divestiture of the major talent agency owned by MCA once that company entered production of movies and television shows, and the Jimmy Stewart *Winchester '73* contract that was negotiated by then super-agent and later powerful head of MCA, Lew Wasserman.

The Stewart contract was the first in Hollywood to promise the star a percentage of a picture's profits. After it was signed, many a talent agent would, over the decades, be able to emulate it and then be able to boast that through application of infinite wisdom, experience, and cunning, they too had managed to extract from the reluctant and greedy studio a piece of the picture's "profits" for their clients. Only later, in the 1980s and 1990s, after exposure of the famous disputes concerning the films *Coming to America* (e.g., see Robb 1990) and *Forrest Gump*, was the real economic and contractual meaning of "profits" more clearly defined and better understood by the Hollywood, Wall Street, legal, and news media communities.[3]

The end of the studio system and the development of the "bankable" star system increasingly enabled stars to command percentages of box-office grosses and was part of an important but subtle shift of economic power that permanently reduced the expected level of aggregate studio profitability (i.e., film industry operating margins). In effect, the great financial bounty that came from the opening of new ancillary markets in cable, DVD, home video, satellite, and worldwide television was largely neutralized, and often fully consumed by rapidly rising compensation to stars of both the human and special-effects kinds.

The history of movie and television accounting has largely reflected these and other changes in the sociopolitical, technological, and industrial structure of the business since its inception in the 1890s. It wasn't until 1973, however, when the American Institute of Certified Public Accountants (AICPA) issued its guide, *Accounting for Motion Picture Films*, that treatments first began coalescing toward uniformity. Before then, it was every movie company for itself, with no way at all to compare the kaleidoscopic financial performance of one studio versus another.

---

[3] *Coming to America*, distributed by Paramount, was one of the highest grossing films of 1988 and the subject of a lawsuit fought in Los Angeles Superior Court over the definition of "profits." An overview of this case is presented, for example, in Weinstein (1998). In the *Forrest Gump* situation, which pertained to one of the top films of 1994, the dispute was over how much of the "profit" should have been paid to the author of the novel on which the story was based. Definitions of profits are discussed in Baumgarten, Farber, and Fleischer (1992); Cones (1997); Daniels, Leedy, and Sills (1998); and Goodell (1998).

The industry at that time was particularly ill equipped from an accounting perspective to adjust to the rapid growth of new sources of ancillary receipts that were starting to come from broadcast television networks, television syndication sales, and the then-embryonic home video and pay cable industries. Indeed, as the licensing of feature films for broadcast television became more frequent and of larger value, the need for new uniform standards in the accounting for television license fees became especially evident. Later on, the same basic notions developed in the aforementioned AICPA guide came to be applied to exhibition licenses granted to cable, syndication, and other such markets. Those basics provide that

1. The license fee (sales price) for each film is known.
2. The cost of each film is known or reasonably determinable.
3. Collectibility of the full license fee is reasonably assured.
4. The licensee accepts the film in accordance with the conditions of the license agreement.
5. The film is available; that is, the right is deliverable by the licensor and exercisable by the licensee.

Of these, the fifth condition, availability, carries the most weight because it is the condition that is controlled by the licensor (i.e., distribution company).

The AICPA rules were then again further refined in the early 1980s, when the FASB issued Statement #53, *Financial Reporting by Producers and Distributors of Motion Picture Films.* The primary consequence was that companies could no longer collectively apply an expense amortization table across all of their releases taken together; they instead had to treat each picture separately and follow stricter guidelines on recognition of revenues and expenses for movies and television productions.

## ACCOUNTING STATEMENT OF POSITION 00–2

Nevertheless, shock waves from the adoption of new distribution and production technologies have continued to necessitate accounting responses by both participants and companies. As home video, pay cable, and foreign revenue opportunities have grown, unions and guilds for actors, directors, producers, writers, stagehands, musicians, electricians, teamsters, and others have asked for adjustments, demanding modified compensation agreements involving a sharing of the additional receipts that flow from the implementation of new technologies. Sometimes, too, the guilds and unions have had to cope with (and are still coping with) downsizing as the rapid pace of innovation involving the application of new skills and methods has replaced older, more labor-intensive ones. Digital film editing and special-effects productions come readily to mind as examples.

Corporations have, moreover, found that changing technologies have made many aspects of Statement #53 obsolete and in need of repair or refreshment. In response, an accounting task force including industry, accounting, and investor representatives was ultimately formed in the 1990s and, after years of debate and comment, Statement #53 was rescinded and replaced in June 2000 with Statement of Position 00–2 (SOP 00–2), *Accounting by Producers and Distributors of Films.* Although this update has largely left the framework established by Statement #53 intact, the prescriptions of SOP 00–2 have tightened some of the Statement #53 reporting requirements for producers and distributors of films, television specials, television series, or similar products that are sold, licensed, or exhibited.

The new rules require, among other things, that

- Exploitation costs are to follow SOP 93–7 (*Reporting on Advertising Costs*), which requires that all marketing and exploitation costs should, for the most part, be expensed as incurred (or the first time that the advertising takes place), with the cost of film prints charged to expense over the period benefited. Previously, such costs had often been capitalized and then amortized over a film's full distribution lifetime.

- Total film revenue estimates against which production costs are amortized are based on estimates over a period not to exceed ten years following the date of the film's initial release, with some limited exceptions. Previously, this period might have been as long as twenty years.

- For episodic television series, ultimate revenue should include estimates of revenue over a period not to exceed ten years from the date of delivery of the first episode or, if still in production, five years from the date of delivery of the most recent episode. Ultimate revenues should include estimates of secondary market revenue for produced episodes only if an entity can demonstrate that *firm* commitments exist and that the episodes can be successfully licensed in the secondary market. Previously, the episodic revenue assumptions were mostly open-ended.

- Syndication revenues for television series episodes are to be recognized over the life of the contract rather than at the first available playdate if certain revenue recognition criteria are not met. Those criteria include the completion, delivery, and immediate availability of the series for exploitation by the licensee and the establishment of a fixed or determinable fee that is reasonably assured of being collectable. For some syndicated series, the effect is to spread the one-period earnings bump previously seen under Statement #53 over more earnings periods.

- Ultimate revenue should include estimates of the portion of the wholesale or retail revenue from an entity's sale of items such as toys and apparel and other merchandise only if the entity can demonstrate a history of earning such revenue from that form of exploitation in similar kinds of films.

- Abandoned-project development costs and certain indirect overhead costs are to be charged directly to the income statement and are thus no longer part of total negative costs – that is, included in a studio's overhead pool.
- Films are to be defined as long-term assets (i.e., as film cost assets), not inventories. This means that their worth is to be based on future cash-flow estimates discounted to present or fair value as compared to the previous condition in which revenue estimates were not discounted. Interest income would be earned as the films pay off.
- If the percentage of unamortized film costs for released films (excluding acquired film libraries) expected to be amortized within three years from the date of the balance sheet is less than 80 percent, additional information regarding the period required to reach an amortization level of 80 percent must be provided.

SOP 00–2 does not fully resolve all controversies, but it nonetheless goes a long way toward standardizing applications of the individual film-forecast method, which has long served as the conceptual foundation of movie-industry accounting. The effects of SOP 00–2 have been notable and noticeable in several respects. Major studios used to have more discretion in when to recognize advertising and marketing costs as an expense; one company's expensing policy could have the effect of depressing profit margins early in a picture's run and of raising them later, whereas another's policy might have resulted in the opposite. Although there is a reasonable case to be made for spreading some promotional and advertising costs over the later markets that stand to benefit from expenditures at the time of initial theatrical release, the new SOP now requires everyone to follow the same method.

The timing of revenue and expense recognition in film accounting is also always complicated by the lengthy nature of the production process, which inevitably turns film "inventories" into long-term assets. Virtually all other businesses define inventories as short-run, meaning they are carried on the books and turned over (i.e., sold) in under a year's time. Statement #53 originally had film inventories grouped into current and noncurrent assets, but SOP 00–2 formally recognizes the special nature of film production by changing the definition of film inventories on corporate balance sheets to unclassified – that is, long-term assets.

Today's balance-sheet footnotes further categorize the inventory as either released or unreleased, completed or in process, with an indication of how much of the costs have not yet been amortized (i.e., expensed by flowing through the income statement). Over the years, companies with the most conservative accounting policies have expensed such unamortized residuals rather quickly, meaning that relatively little remains to be later written off the balance sheet. From Wall Street's perspective, such companies are seen as having high quality-of-earnings reports.

That is not to say, however, that all such residuals ought to be immediately written off. It makes both economic and accounting sense to retain some unamortized residuals because the residuals are the only way to more closely align the timing of revenues received and expenses incurred. As film features typically now earn the bulk of their revenues from nontheatrical sources like home video and DVD, it makes sense to apportion and, therefore, defer chargement of some of the costs involved in making the film to a later date, when most of the revenue is realized in a completed economic transaction and is received by the distributor.

The same also applies to television-program production and distribution. A new and ratings-unproven network series will almost surely involve deficit financings and will thus require fast writedowns of expenses because its prospects for success initially remain highly uncertain. But once the series is on the air for three years and significant syndication revenue potential can be forecasted, the amortization rate is slowed so that some of the ongoing production expense (which usually soars with the popularity of the show's newly developed stars) can be matched against the relatively large additional sources of revenue that are expected to be forthcoming from future syndication sales.

Given all the philosophical and theoretical issues that may be endlessly debated, this approach to writing down filmed entertainment assets is about as good and proper as anything in accounting can be. For, unlike the situation in, say, classical physics, there is no natural law or constant (e.g., water freezes at 32°F) that governs the accounting methodology. Accountants will heuristically agree on a consensus methodology that must by necessity rank implementability and usefulness over theoretical purity.

The methodological faults, though, are perhaps most evident in that feature films and television shows often have an afterlife; they can generate income long after they have been fully expensed (i.e., written down). As such, they then can sometimes become uncommonly profitable assets to own or control, an aspect that is well understood by those who regularly trade in this area.

Still, evaluation of library assets is as much art as science. Introduction of new distribution technologies in the form of home video, DVD, and cable have, for example, historically enabled vast exploitation of such fully amortized assets, and film-industry bookkeeping-system peculiarities have accordingly provided owners with extraordinarily high marginal profits (i.e., all new revenues and no major new costs). Whether the same will happen with Internet distribution is, however, yet an open question.

### THE CORPORATE VIEW

The underlying principle that affects both the corporation's and participants' financial statements stems from the idea that costs and revenues ought to be largely matched in terms of type and timing. This is the basis of modern accrual accounting and is the form followed in virtually all industries, even though critics such as Lev (2001) have suggested that conventional accounting methods do not properly adjust for the changes wrought by the economy's major long-term drift toward provision of services based on intangible assets. In contrast to the situation with immobile tangibles like factory buildings and machinery, balance-sheet valuations tend to become more artful and contentious when dealing with intangibles such software, intellectual property rights, and employment contracts for people who can walk out the door or go on strike.

In corporate accounting for movies and television productions, the central notion is that the company's accounting statement is based on *management's* estimates of the future revenue potential of various projects taken film by film and market by market (e.g., theatrical, video, cable, etc.). These estimates, known as income ultimates because they are projections of what a film might ultimately earn in total from each source, form the revenue basis against which capitalized costs are expensed.

However, because they are a management's estimates – with the estimates being only as good and reliable as the management that makes them – there is sometimes considerable leeway for exaggerations and distortions to creep into the accounting. An aggressive estimate of what might be eventually derived in a cable or syndication sale would, for example, result in the presumption that revenues would be higher than they actually turn out to be. And this would then lead to an overstatement of current or near-term profitability because the company has deferred recognition of some of the total project costs to later periods instead of booking those costs in the current period. Should this occur, the day of reckoning – the day for a writedown – would inevitably arrive once it is seen that actual revenues will be disappointingly lower than had been forecasted. Share prices on the stock exchange have been known to run up or down based on such reports, faulty or not.

The idiosyncrasies of movie accounting also become more visible as we move down a notch from the high corporate overview position to a more contract- and project-specific level. Studio arrangements for production, financing, and distribution (PFD) are normally spelled out in a contract that registers the obligations and compensations to be expected by all parties to the agreement. A studio may, depending on the type of project, be involved in any or all the functions of PFD and marketing.

For their role as gatekeepers and owners of the initial access pipeline to theaters and homes, the major studios are entitled to a distribution fee of some dimension, though whether the typical 30 percent U.S. and 40 percent foreign are the "right" numbers can be forever argued. This distribution fee is earned early in the sequenced stream of receipts and is, thus, relatively sheltered from risk. But, studios will nevertheless continue to bear the considerable risk of losing on theatrical releasing costs even though they normally would be first in line to recoup production, marketing, interest, and overhead expenses. Broadband Internet piracy, wherein a popular film is sometimes on the Net before it is even theatrically released, attacks a studio's income stream at the potentially most valuable and vulnerable point in the entire release sequence: the point at which audience interest and willingness to pay for an admission ticket is usually the highest.

What creative participants rarely seem to fully grasp is that studios have a large and long-term monetary and human-capital commitment to maintain distribution, marketing, and financing capabilities. And this capital commitment must be adequately compensated for its functions or those functions would cease to exist. In fact, despite all of their inherent advantages, studios have often not earned enough to cover their weighted average costs of debt and equity capital (WACC), a situation that modern finance teaches is a prescription for eventual insolvency. In contrast, creative participants all receive for services rendered cashable salary paychecks without whatsoever incurring any capital risks or recurring commitments to continuity.

Indeed, the studio has, in reality, only a few quickly time-perishable slots in which to focus its efforts. In the space of a year, perhaps only forty or so weekends out of the fifty-two are available to attract any sizable audience attention; on the remaining weekends, the target audience is usually otherwise seasonally distracted or in school. Before a PFD contract is signed, literally thousands of potential film projects vie to be produced and then distributed in those scarce slots, of which there are only 220 or so annually (counting the majors) and around 400 if all other film distributors in the United States are included. Meanwhile, each "greenlighted" picture ties up hundreds of individuals, generates thousands of pages of legal documents, and costs many tens of millions of dollars.

## PARTICIPANTS' VIEW

In most businesses, the part of accounting with the fewest misunderstandings and controversies is on the revenue, or sales, line. The buyer exchanges money for the right to license or otherwise use some good or service, and the seller records the sale as receipt of revenue – nothing could be plainer or simpler. Except in the movie business, where, because of the tailor-made contracts and individuality of each project, not every dollar of revenue is created the same as every other dollar of revenue. Here, the murkiness and ambiguity begins, and what happens is gross in more ways than one.

Although it wouldn't characterize anyone with passing familiarity of the movie business, the public at large is often not clear on the difference between box-office gross receipts and the receipts from theatrical rentals that the studio actually receives and recognizes as its revenues.[4] In round numbers, we can generally say that theatrical rentals are about half of the box office, with the other half being retained by exhibitors. Thus, in the beginning, around half of theatrical box-office gross becomes 100 percent of the studio's film rentals. Later in a film's life cycle, gross receipts will also be generated from DVD and home video, pay cable, broadcast television, and other ancillary revenue sources.

---

[4] As discussed in detail in Chapter 5 on exhibition, a movie's box-office receipts are split between the exhibiting theater and the movie's distributor. Because the exhibitor is renting the movie from the distributor, the revenues ceded by the theater owner to the distributor are referred to as "rentals."

Gross comes in many different flavors, and gross participation deals can be generally categorized and ranked from rarest to most common into three basic types: first-dollar, adjusted gross, or gross after breakeven. First-dollar gross participation is available to only a few superstars and, as the name indicates, entitles the participant to receive a share of the studio's first receipts (i.e., 100 percent of the film rentals) after certain limited expenses have been deducted. Adjusted gross is considerably lower down on the pecking order and generally provides the participant with a share of gross receipts after the studio has recouped its negative and print and ad (p & a) costs. And, gross after breakeven, a rung even far lower down, is roughly equivalent to the position of what is loosely referred to as a "net-profit" participant. Here, a participant only shares in gross receipts after the studio has recouped full distribution fees and all costs.

This would be clear enough were it not also for the not-so-minor complication that breakeven also comes in many different variations. What are all the costs and when do they stop being accrued? There are many instances in which a picture in theaters is marginally above "breakeven" but the studio decides to spend more on advertising and sales. The "breakeven" then becomes a "rolling breakeven," a never-reached moving target for some of the lesser participants. Such a rolling breakeven serves the narrow interests of those higher up in the food chain; they would not want it any other way. Additional marketing raises the total gross and the reputations and exposures of the stars. But, just as important, the performance in theaters largely determines, through direct arithmetical links, the prices that the film will be able to command in all of the markets that follow theatrical.

As has been suggested by this brief overview, contract language is the shoal on which participants' ships crash. The words "profit points" or "profit participation" have, for example, probably caused more grief than perhaps any others. The problem is that "profit" in the movie business is not something that follows the ordinary dictionary definition. Profit is instead defined differently in each contract and can mean whatever the parties to the contract define it to mean.

What is perhaps most widely misunderstood is that the "net profit" is really a contingency bonus, which means that if the picture does really well, some of the extra gravy might on rare occasion spill over to the participant – just don't ever count on it happening. Although "gross-profit" participants, theoretically burdened with fewer deductions than those with only "net," might seem to stand a somewhat better chance of seeing income statement daylight, it all depends on the negotiated definitions (which will often require more than five *single-spaced* pages of text to describe). To circumvent many of these problems, studio contracts – in the aftermath of *Coming to America* and other such cases – have begun to use terms other than "profits" to describe the nature of their agreements.

At least a half dozen other key terms also require special care and attention in the crafting of contracts. Of special note are terms such as gross receipts, production costs, and distribution fees, as well as clauses that contain phrases such as "ordinary course of business," the studio "deems," and "follows reasonable and customary practices." Terminology of this type often appears in the deal memo stage, when – for whatever reasons – more specific language has not been negotiated. Such language provides the distributor with ample leeway to make interpretations in its favor, with the vagueness frequently later remedied only through expensive arbitration or litigation.

The media often go wrong in portraying creative talent as being totally naïve and defenseless in negotiating against the presumably rapacious studios. The fact is that almost all contracts are negotiated on both sides by experienced legal and business-affairs representatives who know the score, understand the balance of power, and often switch sides over long careers. Yet, even these professionals can make important exceptions to the contractual studio "boilerplate" only for clients who are in demand – for clients who are truly at that moment stars. As noted previously, the participant takes no capital risk and is not burdened, as the studio always is, by an interest or requirement in maintaining a viable business infrastructure. After the project is finished and the wrap party has folded, the participants are, filmically, gone with the wind.

Although it's virtually impossible, except for superstars, to significantly change or remove many standard clauses and terms from the contracts that are typically offered, the one thing that a participant can be certain of is that, unless challenged, the studio will always interpret such clauses and terms to its financial accounting benefit. It is these (occasionally publicized) challenges by forensic accountants and lawyers working on behalf of their star clients that provide the disciplinary checks and balances needed to keep the playing field level and the system healthy.

Some of the outraged and aggrieved would, with their Hollywood-inflated egos and senses of righteous indignation, nonetheless still argue, "I don't care. Let's sue the bastards and get what they owe us." That, however, is easier said than done. The forensics who conduct such audits are a rather small and well-compensated group that finds it is not normally worth their while to ply their trade in minor cases. Contracts will also usually specify limiting conditions under which an audit is permitted. Although for major cases there is a virtual certainty that meaningful sums will be found, the question for the participant is whether the amount that is so recovered might be sufficient to compensate for the costs in time, money, reputation, and aggravation of bringing suit. Generally, the picture must first do much better than average at the box office to make any such legal action thinkable if not advisable.

Another reason that the situation becomes so quickly convoluted and requires such great legal and accounting expertise is that the studios may not be the participant's worst enemy. The enemies are instead the clauses embedded in the contracts negotiated by representatives of the *other participants!* Perhaps star A is in for a generous cut of gross, however that is defined. That cut will undoubtedly reduce the potential compensation available for lesser stars B, C, D, and so forth. Also, producers will normally be guaranteed a certain minimum payment that must ultimately come out of the picture's defined "net profits," a contractual stipulation that may constrain everyone else's potential payout. Given that they often nurture a project's funding and creative needs over many lean years, producers feel that they are fully entitled to preferential positions relative to those of other participants who much later, and at a far less precarious stage of the project's development, appear on the scene ready to claim the lion's share.

Some of the quirkiest ambiguities also often hinge on definitions and questions surrounding the treatments of various tax credits and remittances, advertising and film-lab rebates, guild fees, licensing costs, and blocked-currency effects. For example, rebates or tax credits might be counted in the distributor's definition of gross receipts. If so, the inference is that the studio's 30 percent distribution fee is applied, thereby leaving that much less available for participants. The alternative would be to use such items as a reduction of the film's negative cost, but then the studio wouldn't earn the larger distribution fee and the overhead and interest charges based on the film's total budget would be less.

For the same reasons, it is important to clearly distinguish between production costs and distribution expenses. When a film is produced pursuant to a PFD deal, the distributor will most likely seek to classify as many expenses as possible as production costs so that such costs will bear overhead and interest. The positions of all participants, including that of the producer, are improved if actual distribution expenses are not classified as production costs. If they are so categorized, then "net profit" participations will be delayed. In negative pickups and pure acquisition deals, however, the opposite classifications are preferred by a distributor seeking to maximize the amount on which distribution service charges may be applied.

Overhead charges that, at least to the participants, appear to be unreasonable expense deductions from their proper share are also frequently disputed. A studio may, for instance, charge 15 percent or more of budget for overhead and may charge a picture for leasing props that could be bought at a local store at much less cost. As a famous producer and comedian once appropriately quipped, the studios charge interest on overhead and overhead on interest – you just can't win.

The home video business, which includes DVDs and videocassettes that are either sold outright (sold-through) or rented to the consumer, has now become so large as to provide for more than half of feature-film-industry profits. It is thus not surprising that contractual frictions involving high-level participants will often be centered on this area.

The home-video business-model configuration, however, differs substantially from that seen on the theatrical side, where the terminology and operating conventions date back to the earliest days of film. Home-video accounting structure instead initially grew out of hybrid recorded music- and book-industry practices in which royalties are paid and advances are earned based on the number of units sold. Here, studios are often able to retain 80 percent or more of wholesale revenues and, in addition, take a distribution fee on those revenues. Participant representatives have long fought to gain a greater share of such revenues for their star clients but have thus far not gained much ground. Understandably, studio negotiators do not yield readily in these matters.

### CONCLUSION

Participants should not come into Hollywood expecting that contract provisions will be governed by fairness and logic. The standard contracts have evolved over a long time and they are not designed to be fair and logical to any individual participant. Yet, in a crudely comprehensive fashion and in the aggregate, there *is* an overall economic logic and fairness to the way in which the system has progressed over the last hundred years. Studios could not perform their collectively valuable functions if their contracts were designed to protect and nurture every grain of sand on the beach. Studio contracts are the way they are so that the whole beach isn't washed away with every risky, exaggerated, or mismanaged project that comes flailing onto the studio's shores. There are always plenty of those. Probably 80 percent of the films that are made don't return the investment in full and, artistic merits aside, the echoes of studio near-death experiences from financially failed pictures like *Cleopatra* (Fox, 1963) or *Heaven's Gate* (United Artists, 1980) still resonate in today's contract terms.

Despite periodic hand-wringing about runaway production and marketing costs that have since 1980 risen at around three times the rate of inflation, the industry hasn't ever been effectively structured to provide broadly based incentives to keep expenses down for long. Those who are consistently serious and powerful champions of budget discipline are not normally applauded or rewarded. And studios must spend money to make money: Cheap doesn't carry far in Hollywood. It never has and it never will.

Indeed, the emergence of new media markets beginning in the 1970s only further fueled the industry's profligacy. Although these opportunities quickly grew large, the increasing cash flows that were so generated ended up being greatly diverted to, among other things, paying stars out of gross receipts and covering the high costs of special effects and marketing. The result: Even with all the new markets that have opened, aggregate industry operating margins as estimated from company 10-K and annual reports (Vogel 2004) are now typically one-third lower than they were in the late 1970s.

To survive over the long term, studios must have sizable financial buffers that can easily support the capital costs, cushion the risks incurred in the normal course of operations, and also provide for a degree of financial flexibility when selecting from competing potential projects.

Accounting for any business is a complex subject shaped by history and culture and technology. The peculiar nature of producing and distributing movies and television shows simply provides an additional twist to a complexity that already exists. Allegations of creative bookkeeping notwithstanding, movie accounting normally involves interpretations of contract terms upon which reasonable and intelligent people can and will disagree.

Bringing a major motion picture to the big screen requires that a vast array of talent and resources be contractually assembled in a limited amount of time. It is a process that will inherently and unavoidably leave in its wake some ambiguities, issues, and conflicts unresolved. Yet, all other things being equal, the best and most important projects will always flow first to those people and studios with the strongest reputations for fair dealing.

It happens that way in every business and in all parts of life.

### REFERENCES

Baumgarten, P. A., D. C. Farber, and M. Fleischer. 1992. *Producing, Financing, and Distributing Film*, 2nd ed. New York: Limelight Editions. (First edition by Drama Book Specialists, New York, in 1973.)

Cones, J. W. 1997. *The Feature Film Distribution Deal: A Critical Analysis.* Carbondale, IL: Southern Illinois University Press.

Daniels, B., D. Leedy, and S. D. Sills. 1998. *Movie Money: Understanding Hollywood's (Creative) Accounting Practices.* Los Angeles: Silman-James.

Dopuch, N., and S. Sunder. 1980. "FASB's Statements on Objectives and Elements of Financial Accounting: A Review," *The Accounting Review*," 55 (January).

Goodell, G. 1998. *Independent Feature Film Production: A Complete Guide from Concept through Distribution.* New York: St. Martin's Griffin.

Lev, B. 2001. *Intangibles: Management, Measurement and Reporting.* Washington, DC: Brookings Institute.

Robb, D. 1990. "Buchwald, Par Experts Wrestle in Profits Bout," *Variety*, June 27.

Vogel, H. L. 2004. *Entertainment Industry Economics*, 6th ed. New York: Cambridge University Press.

Watts, R. L., and J. L. Zimmerman. 1990. "Positive Accounting Theory: A Ten-Year Perspective," *The Accounting Review*, 65 (January).

Weinstein, M. 1998. "Profit-Sharing Contracts in Hollywood: Evolution and Analysis" *Journal of Legal Studies* (January).

# 4

# Theatrical Release and the Launching of Motion Pictures

## CHARLES C. MOUL AND STEVEN M. SHUGAN

When the movie has been made and the costs have been paid, it is time for the distributor to send the movie into the world of potential consumers to find the largest possible audience. Whereas the theatrical life of a movie now represents only one of several revenue-generating components, the launching of a movie has implications that reverberate for the rest of its commercial life. Consequently, this chapter focuses on how movies are sent into theatrical exhibition.

The theatrical release of a movie is the most visible part of its commercial life, and a number of fascinating questions are being or have yet to be addressed. How well can studios and analysts predict movies' theatrical performances? How much is an Oscar nomination worth? Is the current system of release timing the best possible one for consumers? What about for businesses? Is the vertical integration of production and distribution foreclosing independent moviemakers from having their movies shown in theaters? How important is word of mouth, and do distributors anticipate word of mouth and behave in ways to increase their own profits?

This chapter attempts several tasks. First, we examine the movies that were launched in 2002. This was a fairly typical year, and its consideration will instruct later efforts. Second, we integrate a small portion of the extant marketing and economics literature, providing general implications made possible by that integration. The chapter concludes with ideas and directions for future research.

## THE LAUNCHES OF 2002

A proper study of such a topic benefits greatly from observations. We focus our attention on the movies released in 2002. As the case of *My Big Fat Greek Wedding* illustrates, it can be unwise to segment movie releases into low-budget and big-budget categories in advance. We instead use the set of all movies that were released in 2002 and were one of the sixty highest grossing movies in any week during that year. Using this standard and *Variety*'s weekly Top 50 rankings, we observe the theatrical launching of 305 distinct movies over 52 weeks.[1]

We begin our description of the data with a discussion of the available production cost (budget) data and the primary distributors in the sector. We then turn to perhaps the most obvious component of the environment: the seasonality of demand. The discussion then examines how different movies were launched in 2002 once release dates were set. We explore movie quality throughout to give a better sense of trends and patterns. We conclude this section with a look at Oscar launching strategies, advertising and promotion, and other industry practices.

## Budgets

A primary hurdle for an analyst examining the distribution sector is the subjective nature of pre-release consumer expectations. Although it is

---

[1] Five of these were IMAX releases, which may constitute a market distinct from regular format movies. As we discuss, an important aspect of launching movies involves the Academy Awards. Consequently, in certain applications, we include two movies that were nominally released in 2001 to be eligible for that year's Oscars but were more accurately launched in 2002. In those same applications, we exclude a third movie that was nominally released in 2002 but actually launched in 2003.

unlikely that any descriptive statistic will fully capture these expectations, data describing the production budgets of movies launched in a given week might come close for a number of reasons. First, investments should be correlated with returns. Moreover, participants in the production of the movie who are especially talented at making popular movies (e.g., starring cast, director, perhaps even the producers) are likely to command fees approximately in line with their expected contributions. These expenditures are often proportional to marketing expenditures. Additionally, the special-effects expenditures that frequently generate so much of current movies' expected appeal are difficult to capture in any other way. Finally, as in most industries, high-budget projects must, on average, have higher expected returns than lower budget projects.

These advantages might quite understandably be weighed against the cons of the budget's validity (e.g., conflicting numbers from different sources). For example, some of the movie's budget might be wasted and not contribute to the final product.[2] Regardless of these criticisms, the worth of a movie's budget in prediction is an empirical question.

Given these caveats, we assembled budget data for 213 of the 305 movies released in 2002. The primary source was the Internet Movie Database (www.imdb.com), but information from assorted press releases and other Web sources was also used. Budgets in non-U.S. currencies were converted using 2002 exchange rates.

## Distributors

Any look at domestic theatrical distribution should begin with an examination of the distributors. In 2002, forty-four different entities launched at least one movie. For these calculations, the several subsidiaries of a corporation are considered to be single unit (e.g., Buena Vista, Miramax,

---

[2] *Waterworld* (1995) had an estimated budget of $175 million. This included the cost of several sets that sank and had to be rebuilt or were never used.

Table 4.1: *Studio comparison – Domestic theatrical distribution.*

| Distributor | Number of releases | Releases w/budget | Total budget (in $M) | Avg budget (in $M) |
|---|---|---|---|---|
| Alliance | | | | |
| Atlantis | 4 | 3 | 12.75 | 4.25 |
| Artisan | 6 | 4 | 37.50 | 9.38 |
| Disney | 49 | 38 | 1286.25 | 33.85 |
| DreamWorks | 7 | 7 | 413 | 59.00 |
| Fox | 19 | 19 | 602 | 31.68 |
| IDP | 8 | 3 | 10.80 | 3.60 |
| Lions Gate | 16 | 9 | 60.85 | 6.76 |
| MGM | 18 | 11 | 464 | 42.18 |
| Paramount | 25 | 20 | 683.50 | 34.18 |
| Sony | 42 | 33 | 1168.90 | 35.42 |
| ThinkFilm | 4 | 2 | 14.50 | 7.25 |
| Universal | 15 | 13 | 491.60 | 37.82 |
| USA Films | 7 | 5 | 74.14 | 14.83 |
| WB | 40 | 32 | 1502 | 46.94 |

and Dimension are all aggregated into Disney). Because 305 movies were launched that year, it is obvious that at least some distributors are handling more than one release a year. Table 4.1 displays the distributors that released at least four movies in 2002. Disney led the ranks with forty-nine launches, with Sony (i.e., Columbia) and Warner Brothers also releasing a similar number of movies. Paramount, Fox, MGM, Lions Gate, and Universal all released at least fifteen movies. None of the remaining seven entities released more than eight movies.

Although it would be conceivable to further characterize the sector based on each distributor's number of releases, this approach is problematic because the number of releases fails to adequately measure the power of the distributor in the channel and scope of the releases. For example, Lions Gate, despite several releases, has never been considered to be a major player in the industry, at least not on the level of Universal and Fox. In contrast, DreamWorks has increasingly been considered a major player since its arrival in 1997 despite a limited number of releases. To construct an accurate measure of importance in the sector, we consider the sum of the budgets of all movies launched by a distributor in 2002. Although budget data are not available for every movie, the distributor's average budget (also shown in Table 4.1) derived from this measure gives a much more reasonable depiction of the sector.

Eight distributors had an average budget of more than $30 million: Disney, DreamWorks, Fox, MGM, Paramount, Sony (i.e., Columbia), Universal (i.e., MCA), and Warner Brothers. When one recalls that Sony entered into the domestic movie industry by purchasing Tri-Star and Columbia, the cast is virtually the same (with the exception of DreamWorks) as the distributors of the 1930s. USA Films would appear to be the likeliest candidate to break into this group next but, as illustrated by DreamWorks, large and relatively fast movements from newcomers are possible.[3]

The timing of the 2002 launches also indicates that distributors try to space their releases to minimize the potential for one movie to cannibalize sales from another movie also released by that distributor. In thirty of the fifty-two weeks, no distributor launched more than one movie. Closer examination of the other twenty-two weeks gives some indication of why distributors are not more concerned with the prospect of competing with themselves for exhibitors and consumers. In sixteen of those twenty-two weeks, the potential competition from cannibalization was marginal at most, as one movie was a non-English release and the other was a relatively high-budget movie. In four of the remaining six weeks, the overlap was probably minimal because the movies were of such different genres (e.g., *About Schmidt* and *The Lord of the Rings: The Two Towers*). The only real mystery is why Sony chose to

---

[3] An additional way to slice the data would be to consider the cases when studios co-finance a project and split the responsibilities of domestic and foreign theatrical release. Goettler and Leslie (2003) provide both a theoretical and empirical analysis of this strategy.

launch both *Mr. Deeds* and *Men in Black II* in the week of the Independence Day holiday.[4] Given this apparent spreading of product, the idea that distributors cluster their movies to secure more advantageous terms with exhibitors is unlikely to receive any support from the data.

## Seasonality

The release date of a movie is arguably the most difficult decision facing the distributor (Radas and Shugan 1998). The summer season and several holidays are widely considered to be times when consumers (particuarly children) have more free time than usual and are, therefore, especially likely to attend the movies. Having one's movie available during such a time is considered to be a distinct advantage. There is, however, fierce competition among distributors for these peak times, and the competitive disadvantage of high-profile rivals may swamp the perceived advantages. Given the importance of rival distributors' actions, release scheduling is probably the most overtly strategic part of the motion picture launch strategy.

It is easy to see how the perception of seasonal peaks took hold. Box office receipts are typically highest during holiday weeks. To consider weekly trends, we examine the box office of the sixty highest grossing movies, as released by Nielsen EDI and published in *Variety*. Weeks begin on Fridays and end on Thursdays, and holiday weeks are defined as the weeks that include New Year's Day, Memorial Day, Independence Day, Thanksgiving, and Christmas. In 2002, the average nonholiday week brought in about $167 million, while the average holiday week had revenues of $255 million. Indeed, a simple regression of weekly box-office receipts on a dummy variable for these five holiday weeks and an additional dummy

---

[4] The other example of distributor overlap was *Gangs of New York* and *25th Hour*. Both were released on 12/20/02 by Disney but, as we discuss later, this is easily explained by Oscar considerations.

variable for the summer season (Memorial Day to Labor Day) explains a third of the variation in weekly receipts. (Estimated standard errors are beneath the point estimates. Box office [$BO_w$] is in millions of dollars.)

$BO_w =$

$$157.42 + 80.79 * HOLIDAY_w + 34.01 * SUMMER_w + e_w, \quad R^2 = 0.33$$
$$6.88 \qquad 21.65 \qquad\qquad\quad 12.73 \qquad\qquad\qquad\qquad N = 52$$

where
HOLIDAY $= 1$ if the week is a holiday and 0 otherwise.
SUMMER $= 1$ if the week is in the summer and 0 otherwise

Summer appears to add about \$34 million to a week's expected total (when compared to a nonsummer, nonholiday week), whereas a holiday adds just over \$80 million compared to a nonholiday week of the same season. Because the few movies at the top of the rankings can be expected to capture most of this gain, the payoffs from choosing the right release date appear to be impressive.[5]

But are they really? Suppose that distributors believe that holiday and summer releases will be especially lucrative. Given the strategic concerns discussed previously, it seems likely that, in such a world, distributors will release their movies with the highest expectations to coincide with these peak demand periods. So, these statistical results are actually an aggregation of two distinct forces. Holiday weeks have higher receipts in part because of the higher consumer demand that results from more free time and in part because that is when higher expectation movies are released. The statistical trick is disentangling the two effects. One possible tactic would use unpredicted production delays that force release-date delays. We now consider a more modest approach to examine the potential extent of this combination.

---

[5] The often-verified Murphy's Law (named after Art Murphy, longtime industry analyst) states that 20 percent of the movies earn 80 percent of the revenues.

Figure 4.1 illustrates the relationship between a week's total receipts and the largest budget of a movie launched that week for 2002. Figure 4.2 considers a similar relationship, but considers the sum of the budgets of all movies launched in a given week as its budget proxy. Aside from the fact that distributors rarely release a potential blockbuster the week after a major holiday (a tactic that would gain none of the holiday's benefits but all of its competitive downsides), the match is nearly perfect.[6] An extension of this regression should make the point even clearer. Here, we include the sum of the budgets of each week's newly released movies, as well as a similar sum for the previous week. This latter variable helps control for the usual postholiday dearth of new product. (Estimated standard errors are beneath point estimates. Box office $[BO_w]$ and the budget sum figures are both in millions of dollars.)

$$BO_w = 112.76 + 0.20 * BUDGETSUM_w + 0.16 * BUDGETSUM_{w-1}$$
$$\phantom{BO_w = } 13.46 \quad 0.07 \qquad\qquad\qquad 0.07$$
$$\phantom{BO_w = } + 62.96 * HOLIDAY_w + 25.47 * SUMMER_w + e_w, \quad R^2 = 0.48$$
$$\phantom{BO_w = } 20.36 \qquad\qquad\quad 11.64 \qquad\qquad\qquad\qquad N = 52$$

The inclusion of new variables improves the regression's fit substantially but, more important it lowers the estimated impact of being a holiday week (by more than 20 percent) and of being a summer week (by 25 percent). Given the crude nature of the budget variable, it is impossible to accurately say how much of the observed seasonality is driven by the release decisions of distributors. We can, however, safely infer that these endogenous release decisions are causing a substantial part of it.

Recent shifts in release strategies (perhaps caused by changes in the exhibition sector) appear to confirm these empirical findings. Prior to 1996, the conventional wisdom's definition of summer (Memorial Day to Labor Day) that tracked the elementary and secondary school year was

---

[6] Note that this applies only to holidays and not peak seasons.

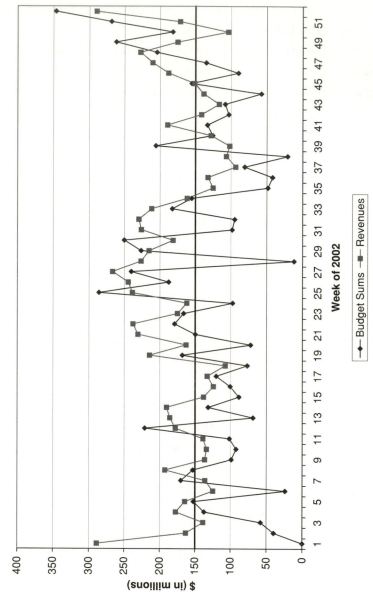

Figure 4.1: Revenues and maximum budget.

88

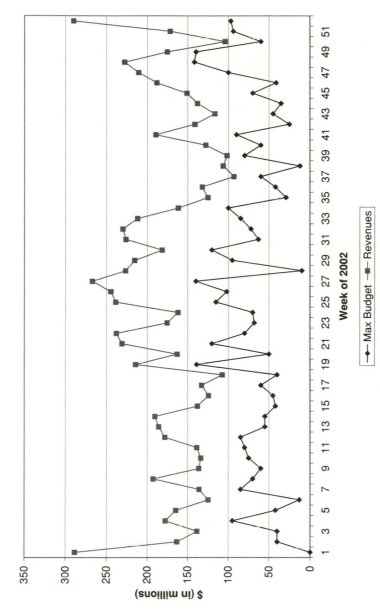

Figure 4.2: Revenues and budget sums.

89

uncontroversial. In 1996, however, *Twister* opened on May 10, two full weeks before the Memorial Day holiday. The $92 million picture ended up grossing almost $242 million in domestic theaters. Nearly $107 million was grossed before the Memorial Day week when *Mission: Impossible* was released. Since then, distributors have been cautiously redefining summer. In 2002, perhaps the most anticipated movie of the summer, *Spiderman*, was released May 3, three weeks before the Memorial Day week and two weeks before *Star Wars Episode II: Attack of the Clones*. Given the competitiveness for choice release dates, it seems only a matter of time before distributors experiment with releases during other traditionally unattractive weeks.

The 2003 release of *Daredevil* on February 14 appears to have been exactly this sort of attempt. It opened on the President's Day holiday and, in a number of ways, resembled a second-tier summer blockbuster: a $75 million budget, a launch on more than 3000 locations, and an opening week of more than $50 million. Similar expansions of what qualifies as an acceptable release date will offer new opportunities to gauge the relative importance of the date versus the movie.

## Release Width

More than three hundred movies were released in 2002, almost six movies per week and more product than most people recognize that the industry offers. This dissonance arises from the fact that many of these movies were launched with minimal fanfare and promptly disappeared from theatrical exhibition. It is tempting to divide movies into big-budget and low-budget groups *ex ante*, where only the former have an opportunity to make a substantial market impact. Cases similar to *My Big Fat Greek Wedding*, however, show that it can be unwise to force such distinctions. As we argue, the theatrical sector is designed to allow the unexpected hit that seemingly comes out of nowhere to become mainstream.

Table 4.2: *Number of exhibiting theaters at launch.*

| Number of launching theaters | | Number | Category | Definition |
|---|---|---|---|---|
| more than 3,000 | 32 | 32 | Very big | more than 3,000 locations |
| 2,501–3,000 | 45 | 122 | Big | more than 1,500 locations |
| 2,001–2,500 | 24 | 46 | Medium | 50–1,500 locations |
| 1,501–2,000 | 21 | 137 | Small | 50 or fewer locations |
| 1,001–1,500 | 10 | 115 | Very small | 25 or fewer locations |
| 501–1,000 | 7 | | | |
| 401–500 | 0 | | | |
| 301–400 | 3 | | | |
| 201–300 | 6 | | | |
| 101–200 | 7 | | | |
| 76–100 | 4 | | | |
| 51–75 | 9 | | | |
| 26–50 | 22 | | | |
| 1–25 | 115 | | | |
| TOTAL | 305 | | | |

As Table 4.2 shows, launches tend to be either large or small. There are relatively few movies that attempt to open at between 50 and 1,500 locations. One explanation of this is that movies themselves are either appropriate or inappropriate for a mainstream audience. If this schism were true, the observed launching split would be intuitive. Our alternative explanation requires slightly more explanation. Indeed, we would like to propose a minor thought experiment.

Imagine that you are faced with the responsibility of distributing movies (for realism's sake, you can assume that you had minimal control over them in production). Each movie has its own level of opening appeal, based on consumer expectations. The expense of releasing a movie at more theaters falls as its expectations are higher. Therefore, it is cheaper to open a high-expectation movie (i.e., a blockbuster) at 3000 locations than to do so for a low-expectation movie (i.e., an art-house picture). Each movie also has its own level of quality. Within this context, you can divide the movies into three groups: those that are worse than expected, those that are better than expected, and those with expectations that are roughly in line with the actual quality. By the statistical nature of this difference, worse-than-expected movies are likely to be higher-expectation movies, and better-than-expected movies are likely to be lower-expectation movies. Your task is to create a distribution system that will maximize the theatrical-run profits for all three types of movies. What would you do?

First, you recognize that you have a limited ability to convey the true quality of the better-than-expected movies to consumers. Being the distributor, your credibility is automatically suspect. For these better-than-expected movies, however, you have a natural ally: consumers who have already seen the movie. Pleasantly surprised moviegoers will share their experience with others, and positive word of mouth spreads. Given this process and the expense of a simultaneous opening at many theaters for such a movie, the ideal approach is to begin with a limited release and then expand to additional theaters as the positive word of mouth increases demand.

Second, you recognize that these limitations regarding your credibility are an asset for movies that are much worse than expected. After seeing such a movie, consumers will tell others not to waste their money, but the original consumers' money will still be in the till. A limited release will cost little but generate little revenue either. A wide release, despite its expense, is the more profitable option because its larger opening will ease the blow of the negative reception.

Finally, you must decide what to do with the movies that manage to meet but not exceed expectations. You could artificially limit the release and then allow the number of exhibiting theaters to expand gradually as viewers confirm to others that their experience was worthwhile. Such a strategy is relatively low-cost, but it forces you to receive your payout over a relatively long time horizon. An alternative would be to let the expectations of the movie determine the width of its opening. This latter option entails higher opening expenses but gives you a large immediate payoff.

Judging between these options is probably a close decision, but one factor clinches the matter. If all movies were either much better or much worse than expected, consumers would eventually be able to distinguish the two based on their different release strategies. You must release the good-as-expected movies in the same way as you release the worse-than-expected movies in order to prevent consumers from discerning the quality difference in advance.[7] The apparent complementarities between advertising and number of locations merely reinforce this story.

And, after this thought experiment, what distribution system remains? One in which launching strategies are largely determined by movies' expectations, but which is also flexible enough to accommodate situations when a movie's quality is substantially different than its expectations. Note that this outcome is different from the one that a benevolent planner would construct. If such a planner were concerned with consumers' opinions after seeing a movie (rather than with profits), all movies would begin with a limited release. Wider releases would be contingent on movies being of sufficient quality. It is interesting to note that this is roughly the system (i.e., movies opening at theaters sequentially rather than simultaneously) that preceded the release of *Jaws* in the summer of 1975. The profit-maximizing release strategy of the thought experiment is a fair characterization of what currently exists. The following three movies from 2002 illustrate these possible outcomes.

The weekly revenue and number of exhibiting locations for *The Count of Monte Cristo* during its lifespan are shown in Figure 4.3. Released January 25, this movie illustrates the case of a movie performing approximately to expectations. The $35 million production was launched at 2,007 locations. Its number of showcases at first grew, presumably as exhibitors switched from played-out holiday movies to fresher fare. This modest increase could not reverse the more structural trend at work, though.

---

[7] This very clean signaling story is muddied by the fact that consumers differ in their preferences (and so a single signal might not be especially informative) and that reviewers already serve this signaling purpose.

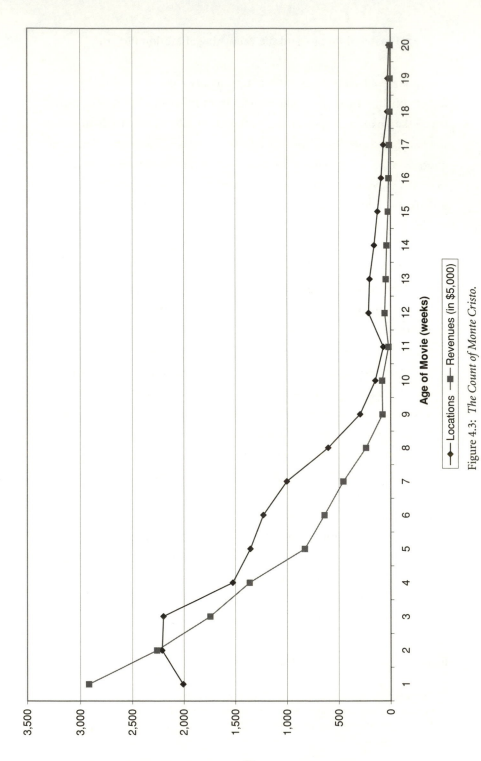

Figure 4.3: *The Count of Monte Cristo.*

94

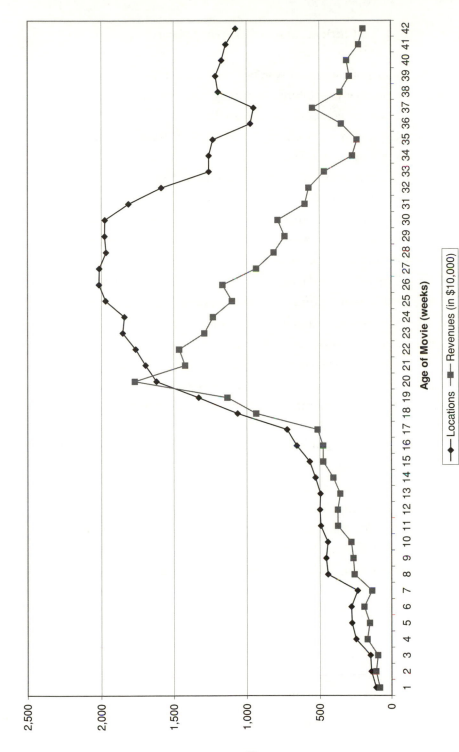

Figure 4.4: *My Big Fat Greek Wedding.*

As the number of consumers who had not yet seen the movie declined, so did the number of exhibiting locations. This reinforced the original effect, and weekly revenues gradually declined.

An examination of *My Big Fat Greek Wedding* (budget: $5 million) is the best way to see how positive word of mouth works in the theatrical sector. The movie's box-office revenues, shown in Figure 4.4, track neatly with the number of locations, with a per-location average of more than $7,200 from its release on April 19 to the week of August 31. At that point, the diminishing returns created by the fact that people tend to see a movie at most once in theaters began to dominate, and from September through January 2003 (when our data end), the per-location average fell to less than $4,300. Despite starting at about hundred locations, the number of exhibiting locations grew to two thousand and stayed there for six weeks. Given the primary demographic of the movie's viewers (people over forty), it seems unlikely that an advertising-intensive and widespread simultaneous launch would have been nearly as successful. As a final note, the upturn in both exhibiting locations and revenues coincides with the Christmas and New Year's Day holidays.

In Figure 4.5 and at the opposite extreme, we consider the $100 million production *The Adventures of Pluto Nash*, the second of three Eddie Murphy vehicles launched in 2002. Even lowered expectations were not in line with the movie's realized quality. Released August 16, the movie's original theatrical run lasted a mere three weeks, with per-location averages of $1,370, $410, and $470 during that time. From the second to the third week, the number of exhibiting locations dropped 86 percent, from 2,320 to 325. On September 20, the movie reappeared on the rankings, but its tenure and impact were both very limited.

With these examples illustrating our understanding of why movies are released in different ways, we next consider what types of movies are launched in which ways. Such an approach requires that we move into the trickier area of quantifying a movie's appeal prior to its release. Our

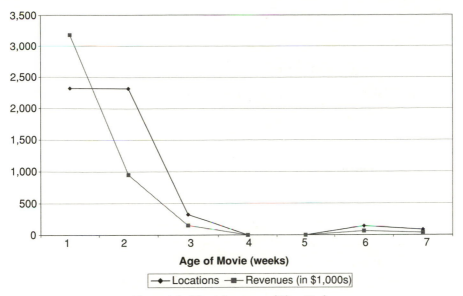

Figure 4.5: *The Adventures of Pluto Nash.*

review of the existing literature discusses several of the methods that have been attempted but, as before, we concentrate our focus on the ability of a movie's budget to predict its launching strategy.

The specific question that we now consider is: What variables predict the width of a movie's launch? We consider both a movie's budget and that budget squared to allow for a nonlinear relationship between the number of launching theaters and the budget.[8] To these two variables, we add an indicator variable for whether the movie was in English (forty-six movies were released in a language other than English.) Finally, we exclude IMAX movies and consider the latter (and more relevant) number

---

[8]  To account for the incompleteness of the budget data, we also constructed an indicator variable for whether a movie's budget was known. Given the inclusion of both Budget and Budget$^2$, this variable had neither a statistically nor an economically significant impact on the number of launching theaters, and results were not substantially changed by excluding it.

of launching theaters for our three Oscar cases. This leaves us with 301 observations.

Let   LOCS = the number of screens at release

  BUDGET = the film's budget in millions of $U.S.

$$LOCS_m = -211.7 + 54.4 * BUDGET_m - 0.26 * BUDGET_m^2$$

  113.8    3.9              0.04

$$+ 565.9 * ENGLISH?_m + e_m$$

  127.4

This estimated equation accounts for about 65 percent ($R^2 = 0.65$) of the observed variation in the number of exhibiting theaters at launch.

The most obvious conclusion is that a movie's budget is a critical determinant of the width of its launch, but this relationship is characterized by diminishing returns, perhaps because of a limited number of available screens. The first $1 million in production costs is expected to secure an additional fifty-four locations, but increasing the budget from $50 million to $51 million is expected to secure only twenty-eight additional locations. From the coefficient on the English-indicator variable, movies in non-English languages can be expected to open at about 560 fewer locations than a movie in English. From an unreported regression, a movie's family status (movies rated G or PG) may have a positive impact on a movie's launching number of locations, but it is not statistically significant.[9]

Recalling the way that movie releases overstated the impact of seasonality, it is worthwhile to consider whether similar factors may be at work with respect to budget's impact on the launching number of theaters. Assume that the industry's highest expectation movies are released at holidays and other peak times. Because the amount of capacity in theaters cannot be changed quickly (except, perhaps, for additional show times), the amount of competition among movies for locations is likely to

---

[9]   Of the 301 launches, 53 were rated G or PG.

be fiercest at these peak times. This can be contrasted with the presumably lower level of competition for locations during the off-peak times. Because higher budget movies are likely to be released during these more competitive times, these regression results that take movies' release dates as given are unlikely to overstate the full impact that a movie's budget has on its launching locations. Were a distributor to release a big-budget blockbuster at an unusual time, such as March or October, it is likely that its budget would have at least as large an impact on the number of theaters at launch than what was estimated because, given less competition, the number of theaters showing the film would increase.

## Oscars

Other than word of mouth, it is not typical for consumers to gain new information about a movie after its release. One notable exception to this is the Academy Awards.[10] Consider the thirty Oscar nominations over the six most prominent categories: Best Picture, Best Director, Best Actor, Best Actress, Best Supporting Actor, and Best Supporting Actress. Of the nominations for movies released in 2001, nineteen went to movies that had been released in December 2001; thirteen went to movies released the week of Christmas or later. This trend is even more pronounced the next year. Of the nominations for movies released in 2002, twenty-four went to movies released in December; eighteen went to movies released the week of Christmas or later.

The Academy does not necessarily respond to these tactics. In 2001, *The Shipping News, Pinero, The Other Side of Heaven,* and *The Royal Tenenbaums* were all snubbed in the major categories despite leaving themselves open to the maximum Oscar bounce with a late December release. The same happened to *Max, Nicholas Nickleby,* and *Narc* in 2002.

---

[10] It is, of course, possible that the effort expended on securing Oscars might not be consumer-driven. Studios might seek Oscars to enhance studio reputations with cast members, directors, and producers.

There are two primary ways in which distributors can leave movies open for the upside of the Oscar announcements. We categorize them as organic and mechanical. The organic Oscar release is the same as the typical strategy for a movie perceived likely to generate good word of mouth: limited opening showcases and gradual expansion. If timed properly, the word of mouth and expansions are still continuing when the Academy announces nominees in mid-February, and the movie benefits from the free publicity and an additional stamp of approval. The mechanical Oscar release follows the letter, if not the spirit, of the Academy's guidelines by opening at the obligatory New York and Los Angeles locations in late December. It may then disappear. It can then either reappear in the data at a date closer to the nominee announcements or, as is common for high-expectation movies, linger at the obligatory theaters for a few weeks and then instantaneously open wide. *Black Hawk Down* is the best example of this latter case from our sample. After opening at four theaters on December 28, 2001, it expanded to sixteen locations on January 11. On January 18, however, it expanded to 3,101 theaters. It is reasonable to believe that this massive expansion represented the movie's true expectations rather than the effect of positive word of mouth. *I Am Sam* (released December 28, 2001) and *Narc* (released December 20, 2002) followed similar, if less dramatic, strategies. *I Am Sam* jumped from one location to 1,281 locations on January 25, and *Narc* expanded from six locations to 822 locations on January 10.

Our previous analysis showed that it can be difficult to separate out the true impact of the environment when distributors and exhibitors simultaneously make endogenous decisions about that environment. Answering the question of how much Oscar announcements (nominees and winners) affect a movie's theatrical demand suffers the same problem. Properly measuring how much an Oscar is worth requires some sort of natural experiment that allows the analyst to distinguish how much box office comes from the fact that the movie is good enough to warrant an Oscar nomination and how much from the nomination itself. Additionally, one must control for the possibility that the week that Oscar nominations are announced is perhaps a high-demand period for all movies.

The Oscar-hopeful movies that were snubbed by the Academy provide a good opportunity to gauge the financial worth of an Oscar nomination. Seven of the movies from 2001 that received nominations were still in theaters when nominees were announced Tuesday, February 12, 2002. Three of the four snubbed movies of that year (*Pinero* had disappeared) were also still in theaters. The seven nominees averaged a 15 percent increase in revenues the week after the announcement, while the three snubbed movies averaged a 46 percent decline that same week. These figures aggregate the effects of consumers responding to the nominations, with the effects of exhibitors expanding or cutting back on the number of locations in response to the same news. Examining per-location averages should give a clearer appreciation of the consumer response to a nomination. By this measure, the seven nominees average just slightly less than the earlier 15 percent increase. The three snubbed movies, however, average no change to per-location average. Although few firm conclusions can be drawn from such a limited sample, it seems clear that exhibitor reactions play an important role in the payoffs from new information.

## Non-Friday Launches

Most movies are released on Fridays. A few movies throughout the year, however, are released on other days, typically Wednesdays. In 2002, seventeen launches occurred on days other than Fridays. The most common explanation is that a release immediately prior to a holiday that falls on a Thursday or Friday allows the movie to be available the entire holiday weekend. Such an explanation accounts for eleven of the seventeen non-Friday launches. Because July 4 fell on a Thursday in 2002 and four-day weekends are common for that particular holiday, the three launches on Wednesday, July 3, definitely fit this pattern. The Thanksgiving holiday also fits this description, and four launches in 2002 occurred on the preceding Wednesday. Finally, four movies were launched on Wednesday December 25. The six exceptions to this holiday rule can be characterized in two groups. The first group includes *Eight Legged Freaks* (launched Wednesday, July 17), *The Good Girl* (launched Wednesday, August 7), and *Femme Fatale* (launched Wednesday, November 6). Possible explanations include attempts to avoid the critic reviews that tend to be released on Fridays or contractual obligations from prior movies that limit exhibitors.

*Star Wars Episode II: Attack of the Clones* (launched Thursday, May 16), *Spy Kids 2: The Island of Lost Dreams* (launched Wednesday, August 7), and *The Lord of the Rings: The Two Towers* (launched Wednesday, December 18) comprise the second group. These sequels may have been perceived to have such pre-release appeal to certain consumers that a Wednesday opening would not suffer from the non-weekend release. Consequently, more typical consumers would be less likely to face sold-out theaters on the weekend. Of course, this is merely speculation . . . many more similar anomalies would be necessary to consider such ideas with any rigor. Survey data from distributors in such cases would obviously be quite useful.

## Advertising and Promotion

In addition to deciding the date and type of launch, the distributor must also advertise and otherwise promote the movie. Advertising on television tends to comprise 55 percent of a movie's advertising budget, with newspapers accounting for an additional 20 percent.[11] Measuring television advertising without information from the distributor is especially difficult because archival records of such advertising are uncommon, and television ad rates vary depending on the program. Anecdotal evidence suggests that the process is heavily front-loaded, and that most advertising is used prior to theatrical release. It is difficult to ascertain these trends, as

---

[11] Galloway (2003).

relatively few movies publicly release their advertising budgets and those that do tend to release cumulative amounts rather than breaking down how advertising is spent over the life of a movie. With these caveats, we gathered advertising budgets of seventy-two movies released in 2002 from various sources.

The median advertising budget of movies for which we could find such data was $25 million.[12] High-budget movies are likelier to have advertising budget data available and tend to have higher advertising budgets. Interpretation of such correlations is difficult. Do high-budget movies have higher advertising budgets because they tend to generate higher expectations and distributors want to convey these expectations? Or do high-budget movies have higher advertising budgets because they tend to be released at peak holidays and face fierce competition from other movies? Perhaps high-budget movies just have larger audiences to reach. There is little consensus on this matter from the empirical literature, and so we bring it up merely as a cautionary observation.

### THE LITERATURE

The marketing and economics literatures now feature many articles involving the motion picture industry (recent examples include Eliashberg, Jonker, Sawhney, and Wieranga 2000; Eliashberg and Shugan 1997; Elberse and Eliashberg 2003; Radas and Shugan 1998; Ravid 1999; Moul 2001). Economists have generally sought to use the industry to illustrate broad economic concepts that are especially important for movies. From a marketing perspective, motion pictures display some of the usual patterns found in other new product categories. Hence, at first blush, textbook marketing principles (e.g., product positioning, target marketing, short-term promotions, market segmentation, etc.) all seem to apply to the motion picture industry. However, motion pictures do have special

---

[12] This compares to the average $30 million advertising budget posted on the MPAA website.

traits that make film launches somewhat unusual. These special traits impact the launching strategy of most motion pictures.

For example, the marketing literature classifies products as either durable (i.e., products where most sales come from first-time purchases) or nondurable (i.e., products where most sales come from repeat purchases). Motion pictures seem to be an unusual and captivating mix of the two types. They appear to be durables because most consumers see a particular movie in theaters only once. However, intent-to-view patterns (described in the next section) associated with box office display a clear nondurable pattern. We discuss why motion pictures possess traits of both durables and nondurables.

To consider these questions and others, we classify the factors that impact the launching strategy of motion pictures into three broad categories: the movie, the buzz, and the environment. The movie category includes the quality of the movie based on various input factors such as the star power of the film. The buzz category includes information such as the film-critic reviews, advertising, word of mouth, and the Internet. The environment category includes variables such as seasonality and competition. As we define it, this last category also includes the role and implications of special characteristics of movie-going behavior (e.g., group decision making). We conclude by discussing the ongoing work to account for the unobserved variables that have plagued empirical work in the area.

## The Movie

This section summarizes research that shows that postproduction predictions, as measured by consumer surveys, accurately predict box-office performance. Preproduction performance predictions, however, are far less accurate. It appears that there is considerable value added during the production process. Unlike new products in other industries where the basic concept is a key predictor of success, the basic concept for a motion picture is far less important. It is the implementation or development of the concept by the new product team (the director, screenwriter, cast, etc.) that is critical.

## Production Factors Influencing Box Office

There appears to be considerable disagreement regarding whether box office is predictable. A series of papers (De Vany and Walls 1996; De Vany and Walls 1997; De Vany and Walls 1999; De Vany and Lee 2002) present statistical evidence that is interpreted as supporting the idea that word of mouth among consumers makes any movie's demand so complex that it is best thought of as a chaotic system. In such a system, William Goldman's comment on the only constant of the industry, "Nobody knows anything," would be precisely true. This branch of the literature concludes that traditional economic analysis of an industry with such characteristics is pointless. Moul (2004a) argues against this interpretation by pointing out that moviegoers' tendency to see a movie in theaters no more than once (i.e., the movie's durability) can generate the same patterns in the data. Consequently, economic analysis that incorporates the durable (no repeat purchases) nature of movies is theoretically sound and should have its worth judged by its results.

Beyond this point, the disagreement on box-office predictability stems to a large extent from a lack of clarity concerning when the prediction is made. There are numerous studies that show that box office is highly correlated with information known before the actual launch of a motion picture (see Austin and Gordon 1987; Dodds and Holbrook 1988; Elberse and Eliashberg 2003; Eliashberg, Jonker, Sawhney, and Wieranga 2000; Hennig-Thurau, Walsh, and Wruck 2001; Neelamegham and Chintagunta 1999; Sawhney and Eliashberg 1996; Smith and Smith 1986; Swami, Eliahsberg, and Weinberg 1999; Zufryden 1996).

A recent study by Chen and Shugan (2002), for example, examines metrics based on various input factors for predicting final cumulative box-office receipts. Based on the theory that team leaders (e.g., directors) make decisions that impact the ultimate project success whereas team members (e.g., screenwriters, cast, etc.) only execute directives, they suggest different impacts on box office from director input and input from other participants. Expected input is based on past performance. For example, a director's past performance consists of the box-office results for past motion pictures by that director. Using such measures, they find it is theoretically and empirically possible to construct a market-based metric for box office based on the past market-level observations of the members of the team producing the movie. The average past performance of the director is the best predictor of the box-office performance for the director's most recent film. However, the maximum past performance is a better predictor for team members other than the director. Hence, when forecasting, the director should be partially penalized for poor past box-office results, whereas the other team members should not.

Despite strong correlations, Chen and Shugan (2002) find that their models can explain only one third of the variation in box office. These are similar to other studies in the literature (e.g., Sawhney and Eliashberg 1996). Hence, the news is mixed. Certainly, it is possible to predict the box office before production begins; however, those predictions are not sufficiently accurate to predict theatrical success. That time, of course, is the point when most resources are committed. Motion pictures create a special problem not encountered in the general new product literature. Because the basic concept is not critical, initial market research provides less useful guidance. Moreover, the nature of the production process prevents continuous feedback through market research to refine the product during the development process.

Moul (2004b, 2004c) uses similar measures of cast and director appeal to decompose movie fixed effects from a variety of demand specifications, including several discrete-choice models. The discrete-choice models that have become common in industrial organization and marketing are ideal for the movie industry. These models assume that consumers see, at most, one movie in theaters each week and that each consumer chooses her favorite option (including the option of seeing no movie). Consumer behavior that depends on movie-specific characteristics as well as the number of exhibiting theaters and advertising[13] can then be identified from the available aggregate data. Moul (2004b) uses these models to identify the situations when a movie's age sufficiently captures the decay in a movie's theatrical demand and when a variable of past sales provides additional and valuable information. Although the various models' fit to the data is generally good, most of this stems from exploiting the movie dummy variables and (when available) the observed levels of exhibition and advertising. When these screening and advertising variables are excluded and absorbed into the movie effects, the prediction accuracy of the best model is approximately the same as Chen and Shugan's (2002).

The competitive environment that a movie faces is also an important consideration. A key finding from the demand estimates of Moul (2004c) is the statistical confirmation that, although action movies and family movies both tend to perform well at the box office, the genres achieve this in different ways. The data suggest that consumers' general preference for action over non-action movies is relatively weak and that there exists a set of consumers (e.g., teenage boys) with strong preferences on the action versus non-action issue. This contrasts sharply with the case of family movies. The typical moviegoer has a substantial preference for non-family movies – that is, a strong distaste for such features. Family movies perform well because a subset of consumers (e.g., families) has markedly different preferences than the average consumer, and relatively few family movies are released. It is this typically weak competition in what is apparently a niche market that has driven the profitability of kid-friendly fare.

These results are theoretically robust to the unobserved characteristics that dominate the movie industry. The importance of a movie's unobservable characteristics, however, changes dramatically after the movie is made. At that point, predictions that exploit potential advance

---

[13] Moul (2004b, 2004c) uses a weighted average of column-inches of advertising in the Friday *New York Times* and the Sunday *Chicago Tribune* as a proxy for total advertising expenditures.

viewings become far more accurate. Although there remain random shocks in the environment that impact box office, the most important factor determining box office – i.e., the film quality itself – is fixed.

### Questionnaires Can Predict Pre-Launch Success

Although useful mathematical models have been developed to forecast the box office of movies shortly after release, these models depend on box-office data that are not available pre-release. Pre-release forecasting has remained an important problem. To forecast the box office of a motion picture before its release, Shugan and Swait (2000) use two sources of information about the movie. The first source is the aforementioned forecast based on the prior history of other movies that involved some or all of the same cast members, directors, producers, and screenwriters. The second source of information is the stated intent-to-view measures provided by respondents who were given information about the film. The intentions were scored on a nine-point scale varying from definitely will not see (1 out of 9) to definitely will see (9 out of 9).

After providing respondents with information about the movie (e.g., script synopsis, trailer, participants), respondents use the nine-point scale to gauge their likelihood of viewing the movie. Shugan and Swait (2000) then develop a model that links intent-to-view measures with ultimate box-office performance. Because of the various feedback effects of screening intensity and advertising, a movie with a wide launch that does not open strongly is unlikely to ever attain much of an audience. The best predictor of a movie's performance is, therefore, based on the percentage of very enthusiastic scores rather than the average score. Low and Moderate scores both produce similar behavior.

This result is borne out in their data. Figure 4.6 shows the distribution of intent measures for the movie *Beavis and Butt-Head Do America*. Note that there are many more people who would never see the movie than people who would definitely see it. The mean intent-to-view score is about 5. Neither description seems promising. The movie, however, had an

**Frequency**

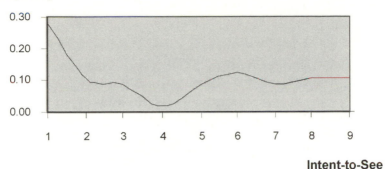

**Intent-to-See**

Figure 4.6: Distribution of intent measures for *Beavis and Butt-Head Do America*.

impressive box office of $63 million. The reason for this was the number of very high intent scores. More than 20 percent of the respondents scored the movie as an 8 or 9 in the intent-to-view survey. This can be contrasted with the distribution of intent-to-view scores for *McHale's Navy* in Figure 4.7. Although this movie had approximately the same average intent-to-view score, it lacked the enthusiastic responses. This absence was apparent in the final box office, as *McHale's Navy* completed its theatrical gross with $4.4 million.

It is curious that the mean intent-to-purchase score should predict moviegoer behavior so poorly, because the mean score typically predicts consumer behavior well for durable products. In this respect, movies appear to more akin to nondurable packaged goods. Shugan and Swait (2000) use this insight by incorporating averages of a fourth-order polynomial of the intent-to-view measures (i.e., $Intent^2$, $Intent^3$, $Intent^4$) to explain what the parameters of Chen and Shugan (2002) could not. By incorporating these intent-to-view measures, they explain 63 percent of the variation in cumulative box office, a vast improvement over the 33 percent from Chen and Shugan (2002) alone. This quality of prediction makes the application of traditional marketing strategies feasible and, consequently, emphasizes the value of both intent-to-view measures and the movie trailer.

**Frequency**

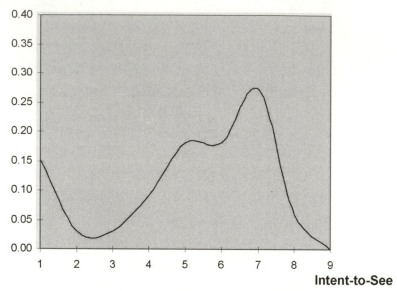

Figure 4.7: Distribution of intent measures for *McHale's Navy*.

## The Role of Star Power

Traditionally, the marketing literatures on both durable goods and non-durable/packaged goods agree that branding is one of the more important determinants of the success of new products. The brand name provides reputation, which in turn makes seller statements about new products more credible. Such credibility is critical to obtaining initial trial and ultimately to achieving a new product's success.

For packaged goods, firms have a greater incentive to match buyer preferences with actual product attributes to ensure repeat purchases. This provides a mechanism for buyers to punish misleading firms. Buyers who were misled merely avoid repeat purchases, making the initial purchases of advertising unprofitable. Durable goods, however, lack that punishment mechanism, and it is here, where buyers have no recourse for bad quality, that branding is particularly important. Branding provides needed credibility because the firm has an incentive to maintain the value of the brand name. Under this scenario, buyers can punish the firm by not purchasing other products offered under the same brand name.

Branding is conspicuously absent from both production and distribution in the motion picture industry. With a few exceptions (e.g., Pixar and Disney movies for children and families), most motion pictures fail to create significant links to the studios, distributors, and exhibitors who promote the movies. The only reputations that seem to be at work are those of the cast, the property (e.g., the book, play, or comic book), and, to a lesser extent, the director.

Given that most moviegoers are young adults with little knowledge of directors' reputations and few properties are well known, star power becomes the only possible source of branding. Empirical research generally views star power as one of the four most important determinants of motion picture box office; the other three are the budget, the director, and the number of opening screens (Litman 1983; Litman and Kohl 1989; Litman and Ahn 1998; Prag and Cassavant 1994; Wallace, Siegerman, and Holbrook 1993; Zufryden 2000; Elberse and Eliashberg 2003). We next consider stars as a form of branding, as well as the cost of stars and whether that cost is justified. We conclude with perhaps the most concrete advantage of star power: free ink.

*Type of Branding.* It is important to note that, although box office is a one-dimensional measure of quality from the firm's perspective, the branding problem is different. In many product categories, there are numerous products for different product customer types. Products can differ in design, flavor, color, options, style, stain, motif, features, and layout (Bergen, Dutta, and Shugan 1996). From the point of view of the customer, branding allows matching of tastes rather than merely providing a one-dimensional measure of quality.

Star power could theoretically perform the same function. A star associated with particular movie attributes (e.g., action, romance, etc.)

could provide a strong signal. The presence of the star could also signal the level of those attributes. Moreover, the high salary of a star, the star's possible participation in the profits of the movie, and other costly benefits to procure the star could provide some credibility to claims involving substantial attention to the movie. At a minimum, these facts signal that the studio and producers have large investments in the movie. A large investment might suggest a greater probability of a great film in the corresponding genre – an outcome that is, of course, by no means certain.

It is unlikely, however, that star power can provide a full substitute for branding. First, the star cast members usually have little control over the creative content and editing of the movie. Although some stars can challenge directors, it is unclear whether great acting corresponds to superior script writing and money-making directing. For branding to be credible, the branding firm must have the resources to produce the consistent qualities associated with the brand name. Given that stars work for different studios and different directors and participate in different movies with very different budgets, this consistency is hardly guaranteed.

There is still another reason why it is unlikely that stars provide real branding. To be effective at branding, a star needs to have a substantial part of her reputation at stake on the movie's success and the star must be able to ensure that reputation. Moviegoers, for example, must know that if the star is disappointed in the movie, she has the ability to withdraw support for the movie.

Contracts, however, are made well before production begins. As discussed, the true quality of the movie is unknown at that point. Once the quality of the movie is known, the star has no easy method for withdrawing from a disappointing movie. Hence, the star is unable to provide a credible guarantee of quality. Although stars can refuse to participate in obviously low-quality projects, the star has insufficient information to implement an effective branding strategy at the time that contracts are signed.

## The Real Benefit of Stars – Free Ink

Although star power is usually associated with the branding effect, an often-overlooked advantage of star power is promotional effort, often called "free ink." Using cast members to promote movies provides an extraordinarily cost-effective method of getting free advertising and publicity for a new movie.

Many talk shows, entertainment shows, and semi-news shows will provide free airtime to interview the stars of upcoming features. From this perspective and unlike most other product categories, new motion pictures are themselves news. A typical 30-second advertising spot on a popular show like "The Tonight Show with Jay Leno" (NBC) can cost $60,000. A star with a new movie can easily generate 15 minutes of publicity for the movie on a popular talk show at a value of $1.8 million. "The Tonight Show" is especially useful for research purposes, as it maintains for public use an episode guide that includes past guests. On the 169 new episodes that aired from December 2001 through September 2002, 118 guests had a still-in-theaters movie or a new release within the next four weeks. Big-budget movies typically promoted with more than one guest. *Men in Black II*, for example, had a different cast member on the show for each of the five nights of the week beginning Monday, June 24. Although less visible movies also use the platform, their potential to do so appears to depend on the celebrity of the actors. For instance, *The Importance of Being Earnest* (released May 17, 2002) opened at only thirty-eight locations, but Reese Witherspoon promoted it on "The Tonight Show" two days before.

In addition to talk-show appearances, distributors and studios can cajole movie critics using interviews with stars as inducements. Cooperative critics (those who avoid very negative reviews) can gain access to these stars for interviews, whereas other critics are denied access. In this way, stars become important tools for the studios in influencing reviews.

The trailers themselves become valuable publicity vehicles when they contain stars. Similar to music videos, trailers are seen as somewhere between content and advertising. It is possible that the audiences for many movie-critic television shows are as interested in seeing the trailers as hearing the reviews. Moreover, many entertainment programs will air a trailer that contains well-known cast members without charge.

Finally, merchandising deals and co-advertising arrangements (e.g., with fast-food franchises such as McDonald's and Taco Bell) are made possible in part by having stars in the movie. The prevalence and value of these deals have weakened somewhat after *Star Wars I: The Phantom Menace*, which was widely considered to be an overkill disaster on the merchandisers' part.[14] For the 2002 releases, we were able to find such tie-ins for eight movies. McDonald's has an exclusive relationship with Disney, and helped promote *Lilo & Stitch, Treasure Planet*, and the live-action *Pinocchio*. Burger King promoted *Ice Age, Spirit: Stallion of the Cimmaron*, and *Men in Black II*. Such promotions focused on toys inspired by the movie. As such, it is not surprising that these tie-ins emphasize movies targeted at younger movie viewers. Like the budget, the stars might signal commitment, but their more valuable function might be to provide opportunities for merchandising.

## The Buzz

### *The Role of Critical Reviews*

Product reviews exist in many product categories and provide a source of third-party evaluative information (e.g., Eliashberg and Shugan 1997). Such information about key product attributes (Shugan 1980) is indispensable for early adopters who buy when less information is known (Allenby, Jen, and Leone 1996) and later buyers who make more informed compromises (Kivetz and Simonson 2000). Furthermore, recent technological advances (Kent and Allen 1994; Hoffman and Novak 1996) have created an explosion of product-related information. Advances

---

[14] *BusinessWeek*, 6/3/02.

in computer-search technology, relational databases, and Internet commerce are combining to provide moviegoers with more evaluative information than at any prior time in history (Alba et al 1997).

Studios and distributors have watched the growth of evaluative information with trepidation. Before the growth of these new technologies, intensive advertising and other quality signals (Rust and Oliver 1994; Kirmani and Rao 2000) have traditionally overwhelmed third-party evaluative information (Eliashberg and Shugan 1997). That situation, however, is changing.

This section discusses four aspects of critical reviews: distinguishing predictor and influencer effects, the different types of critics and their respective incentives, the ability of studios and distributors to influence their evaluations, and the diagnostic value of third-party information.

### Influencers or Predictors?

The favorability of critical reviews tends to be positively correlated with how well a movie does at the box-office. How much of this is because critics, like everyone else, prefer higher quality movies (i.e., critics predict)? And how much of this is because moviegoers respond to critics' reviews (i.e., critics' influence)? Eliashberg and Shugan (1997) first tried to separate these two impacts that critical reviews have on box-office success. Using a sample of fifty-six long-running movies released in the early 1990s, the authors regress weekly box-office revenue on the movie's percentage of positive reviews for each of the first eight weeks of a movie's run. They find that the percentage of positive reviews is only marginally significant during the first four weeks of the movie's run; the effect becomes larger and more significant during the next four weeks. Based on their maintained assumption that the influence effect declines over a movie's run, the authors conclude that the influence effect cannot be important and must be dominated by the prediction effect.

Reinstein and Snyder (2004) use a different approach to separate the two effects and reach a different conclusion. They specifically examine the impacts of the televised opinions of Gene Siskel and Roger Ebert on opening weekend revenues for 609 widely released movies.[15] The authors approach the matter by taking advantage of the fact that 19 percent of movie reviews by Siskel and Ebert aired after the movies' opening weekends. By assuming that this 19 percent was selected randomly, they conclude that the influence effect of those reviews was substantial. Specifically, their estimates suggest that a movie that received two thumbs up would gross about 33 percent more in its opening weekend than if the same movie had received two thumbs down. Although these estimates include all feedback effects (e.g., additional advertising prompted by the favorable review) as well as the direct effect, these conclusions are sufficiently large that they warrant further examination of their model's key assumption. We return to this topic in our discussion of biases in critics' reviews.

### Different Types of Critics

Shugan and Winner (2002) classify third-party suppliers of information into three types. The type of review depends on the source of revenues employed by the reviewer. The reviewer might supply reviews based on personal incentives (type 1), revenue from moviegoers (type 2), or revenue from studios/distributors (type 3).

**1. The reviewer lacking reputation**: Type 1 reviewers usually distribute information on the Internet. They can be anonymous and, even if they reveal their names, they lack established personal reputations. A reader of these reviews can only judge the credibility of the review by its contents rather than by the history of past reviews. It is, consequently, difficult for readers to judge the motives of type 1 reviewers. As Shugan and Winner (2002) note, these reviewers often communicate on Web message-boards using pseudonyms, and their reviews

---

[15] Agresti and Winner (1997) found that, of eight of the most popular reviewers in the United States in 1997, Siskel and Ebert had the strongest agreement.

are frequently negative. Given the potential identities of such reviewers (e.g., clandestine studios trying to promote their own movies or to damage the competition, disgruntled employees or fans) and the subsequent difficulties consumers have in assessing reliability, many of these reviews might have little impact (Pack 1999).

**2. The independent reviewer who accepts no advertising revenue**: Type 2 reviewers obtain revenue directly from potential buyers. For example, revenue might come from subscriptions or direct fees for the review itself. These reviews must constantly maintain a reputation for quality to ensure future revenues. Traditional reviewers of this type include *Consumer Reports* and movie reviewers who make substantial revenue from syndicated columns and movie guide sales. To maintain a significant distance between this reviewer and the seller of the product being reviewed, advertising revenue from the seller is often forgone. Sources with many independent and one-time reviewers (e.g., http://www.rottentomatoes.com) are far more negative than sources with primarily professional reviewers (e.g., *Entertainment Weekly, Variety*). Although potentially profitable, this reviewer type is relatively rare. As evidenced by *Consumer Reports*, it is difficult to ensure that evaluative information is not freely disseminated in the market (Dougherty 1983; Knowlton 1998).

**3. The professional reviewer who accepts advertising revenue**: Type 3 reviewers accept considerable financial support from sellers. Although this reviewer must maintain a reputation for honest reviews, he or she obtains revenue from potential buyers and advertising revenue from the sellers of the reviewed products. Despite this conflict, this reviewer type is both very common and growing.

### Influences on Critic Evaluations

Using data collected from *Variety*, Shugan and Winner (2002) compare professional reviews with independent reviews. They find that a magazine that accepts advertising is as likely to be negative toward a particular movie as a magazine that does not accept advertising. They also find, however, that magazines that accept advertising are more likely to be positive about a movie than magazines that do not. Magazines that accept advertising do not review movies that would have received negative reviews; they instead do features on the movie or interview a star of the movie. This indicates a strong relationship between the quality of the motion picture and the number of reviews appearing in magazines that accept advertising from distributors and studios.

Because most reviewers consider only a small fraction of all movies that are widely released, advertising can apparently discourage some reviewers from writing on movies that would receive negative reviews. There are other ways to influence critics as well. Some distributors and studios wine and dine critics at previews. Cooperative critics are introduced to the stars and granted interviews. The studios can promote critics by quoting them in the studio's promotional literature. Finally, studios can simply avoid inviting hostile critics to previews.

Many studios and distributors arrange advance screenings for critics so that their reviews can appear in a timely fashion at or before the movie's launch. If negative reviews are expected, however, the studio may decide not to screen a picture in advance, thereby delaying the bad news. If this tactic is widespread enough, then the estimation strategy used in Reinstein and Snyder (2004) is invalid, and estimates would be biased towards overstating the influence effect. More explicit treatment of when movies are reviewed is needed for future natural experiments on the topic.

### Diagnostic Value

Eliashberg and Shugan (1997) argue that, rather than fearing movie critics, studios and distributors might consider critics as leading indicators of a movie's eventual success. Although studios and distributors might dislike negative reviews, these reviews could be important diagnostic predictors that help avoid a disastrous release. Negative reviewers could suggest the need for better positioning, distribution, and editing strategies. Although Warner Brothers declined to allow critics to preview *On Deadly Ground* for fear of negative reviews, the movie was still terribly unsuccessful at the box office. Had Warner Brothers previewed the motion picture, the negative reviews might have led the studio to reconsider the immediate launch and instead obtain more market research and revise its distribution strategy.

## The Role of Advertising: Advertising and Word-of-Mouth Effects

Many marketing articles have investigated the diffusion patterns of new products (e.g., Mahajan, Muller, and Bass 1995). A key finding is that the sales life cycle for most durable goods is a quadratic shape. Consider Figure 4.8, which shows a typical durable diffusion pattern. Note that sales grow from a starting point well above zero, reach a peak, and then asymptotically decline to zero. Mathematically, this diffusion pattern is captured by the following equation:

$$\frac{f(T)}{1 - F(T)} = p + q F(T)$$

where

$f(T) =$ density function for unit sales (i.e., sales in continuous time divided by market size)

$F(T) =$ cumulative distribution function for unit sales

$p =$ parameter capturing sales independent of word of mouth (e.g., advertising)

$q =$ parameter capturing the magnitude of word-of-mouth effects

It is well established that, as positive word-of-mouth effects decrease, the diffusion curve grows flatter. Figure 4.9 illustrates different magnitudes of positive word of mouth, denoted by the $q$ parameter. All of the curves have the same market size (i.e., area under the curve). All of the curves also have the same innovative parameter $p$. Hence, all curves start

**Diffusion Pattern (Small *p*)**

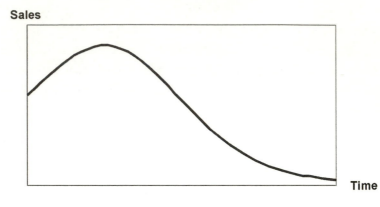

**Diffusion Pattern (Large *p*)**

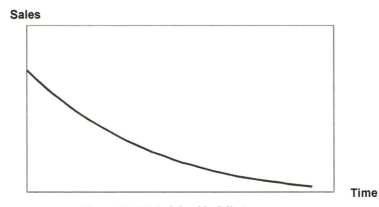

Figure 4.8: Typical durable diffusion patterns.

at the same point before word of mouth begins. Positive word of mouth has little or no impact on the first-week sales but instead moves sales from later periods to earlier periods.

In contrast to nearly every other durable good, the motion picture industry seldom observes these patterns for box-office sales. More frequently, box office starts high and declines steadily over time. This pattern is typical regardless of the success (e.g., the successful *Terminator II* versus

**Sales**

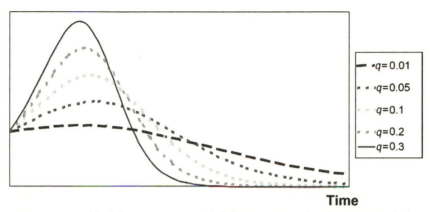

Figure 4.9: Durable diffusion patterns with different magnitudes of positive word of mouth.

the unsuccessful *Intersection*) and the reviews (e.g., the favorably reviewed *City Slickers* versus the unfavorably reviewed *Battlefield Earth*). Radas and Shugan (1998) show that in some cases it is necessary to adjust for seasonality to uncover this underlying pattern.

The typical box-office pattern over time for most movies can, however, be consistent with standard diffusion models for durable goods. This fit requires that factors that determine sales other than word of mouth, factors such as advertising, have dominating effects. Figure 4.10 shows the impact of changes to the $p$ parameter on the shape of the diffusion curve. The only case that produces the most common pattern for motion pictures is the case where advertising completely overwhelms word-of-mouth effects. The implication is that the industry has adopted a strategy of overwhelming post-release word of mouth with heavy promotion including advertising, trailers, and star appearances. Finally, Radas and Shugan (1998) show that most advertising appears to accelerate the time at which box office is collected rather than increasing its total size. They note that this finding may only hold with movies that display positive rather than negative word-of-mouth effects.

**Sales**

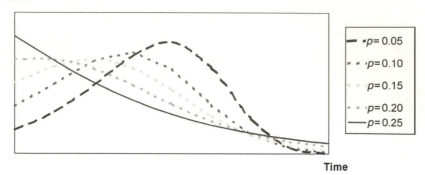

Figure 4.10: Durable diffusion patterns with different magnitudes of non–word of mouth.

The heavy promotion strategy adopted by the studios is puzzling for several reasons. First, as the next section discusses, television and related advertising media are inefficient for most movies, given their limited audience. Second, the life of most movies is usually only several months, so heavy promotion might not be justified if all it accomplishes is moving box office forward by several weeks. Finally, although the studio-distributor share of the box office (discussed in detail in Chapter 5) is higher during the first few weeks, that percentage is negotiable. It would be cheaper to change the sharing of revenue rather than spend massive amounts on advertising.

### Advertising to a Limited Audience

Most studies would consider a theatrical box office of $60 million as an acceptable performance for a movie with an average budget. An outstanding movie might gross $100 million at theaters. Considering a ticket price of $6–8, fewer than 9 million people see a good movie, and 14 million people see an outstanding movie. Although these numbers appear large, McDonald's serves 46 million customers each day. Starbucks claims to have 7 million customers daily. "The Tonight Show with Jay Leno" attracts 5.7 million viewers per night. Compared to these measures, the audience for a typical movie is rather small. Moreover, there is little opportunity to gain future sales from repeat purchases. Advertising on mass media is relatively ineffective because most of the audience is not in the target market. Additionally, as our intent-to-view survey shows, only the very enthusiastic moviegoer will see a movie. To be effective, advertising must convert the moderately enthusiastic to the very enthusiastic. For these reasons, targeted advertising appears to be far more effective. Theatrical trailers naturally target movie-going audiences. Similarly, posters and other promotional items are very effective when employed at the theater.

Unfortunately, the market research necessary for accurate targeting is usually unavailable because traditional market research requires trailers that are available only after a movie is complete. If more than teaser trailers during early production phases become technologically feasible, market research might not only target advertising effectively but also impact the design of the movie itself. Given the current state of technology, though, the durable nature of movies and their consequent short theatrical lifespan limit the ability of distributors to change an advertising strategy and reposition a movie to a new audience.

### The Trailer

The trailer (named because they originally trailed feature attractions) remains a fascinating aspect of motion pictures. There are often eight trailers for every slot before a feature presentation. Studios and distributors are well aware of their importance. Whereas early trailers were made by studios, trailer production houses today make most of the product. Trailer production now goes through a series of stages. The first stage is a teaser that merely reveals the script synopsis and information about the cast and director. The second phase is a trailer with apparent scenes from the movie. The final trailer often provides the story line with scenes in a scripted sequence. Although there might be some marketing logic behind this strategy, an alternative explanation is that the sequence is constrained by production. Given that rush footage is not suited for general viewing, each trailer might represent all that is possible at each point in time, given the state of production. This is a testable hypothesis because both trailer dates and production dates are published.

Recall that first-weekend box office is highly correlated with cumulative box office, and the role of critics as influencers is uncertain. Given these findings, it may be that the movie trailer is not only the single most important influence on moviegoers but the only significant one. This is consistent with the high correlation between cumulative box-office performance and intent-to-view measures. Trailers are, indeed, a free sample that determines the product's ultimate path.

It is interesting to note that, unlike other free samples, moviegoers know that the trailer is biased and presumably represents only the best scenes of the movie. Nevertheless, using primarily this biased information, moviegoers appear to anchor their judgments and make appropriate decisions. This fact, indicating that consumers can be very sophisticated when filtering information, might have important implications for the advertising of other products.

## The Environment

### Summer and Holidays

As shown in our examination of the box office through 2002, the magnitude and influence of seasonality on motion pictures and other entertainment products appear to be extraordinary. Holidays certainly have two potential effects. For some movies (e.g., children's), these times might suddenly increase the market size because children are unable to see motion pictures during school days. Holidays can also change the composition of the market (e.g., from dating couples to families). Although it remains unclear why weekends alone would be insufficient to support all family-oriented movies launched during the school year, holidays might temporarily increase primary demand.

In contrast, holidays might merely accelerate the box office. If the potential market for a particular movie might be almost fixed, a holiday might condense several weekends into single holiday period. Supporting this idea, exhibitors observe a large trough after the holiday period. Because market expansion is far superior to market acceleration, this is a very important issue that awaits future research.

Einav (2003a) uses a discrete-choice model of consumer demand to better gauge the true impacts of seasonality. This model is based on the demand for a movie falling as it ages, and this distaste for age also captures the typical effect of declining numbers of exhibiting theaters and of decreasing advertising over a movie's theatrical life. By first estimating movie quality levels that fit the data, he is able to disaggregate the gross seasonality from the underlying seasonality. This approach is analogous to but far more sophisticated than our inclusion of budget data when examining the releases of 2002. The primary finding is that underlying seasonal effects are much smaller and quite different from the observed pattern of sales. Such a finding calls into question the common practice of observing seasonality by simply examining sales.

## *Competition*

The movies that consumers have as options are clearly an important aspect of the environment. Krider and Weinberg (1998) show that studios often avoid direct competition by not releasing competing movies on the same weekend. These results parallel our findings from the launches of 2002. Their theoretical analysis suggests that weaker movies should delay openings rather than opening simultaneous with stronger movies, and their statistical evidence on launching behavior from the 1990 summer is consistent with that model. Ainslie, Dreze, and Zufryden (2003) find additional and strong support for those findings.

Einav (2003b) uses his earlier demand-side estimates to approach a similar question. Using his estimates of underlying seasonality, he finds that distributors "over-cluster" their releases: too many high-quality movies at high-demand times and too few at relatively low-demand times. Industry profits could be increased by spreading movies more evenly throughout the year. Although competing distributors would not necessarily act to maximize collective profits, the extent of the departure of observed releases from various theories leads the author to posit a number of noneconomic (e.g., ego, extreme risk aversion) explanations. Corts (2001) focuses attention on how distributors' decisions are affected by the fact that they have a portfolio of movies to launch. Examining all movies that were widely released in 1995 and 1996, he finds that different distribution arms of the same company act as integrated parts of the studio and also that current allocative systems do not achieve efficient scheduling outcomes. Neither analysis, however, considers the role of ancillary markets in distributors' decisions; consequently, rich opportunities for future research on this topic still exist.

These results suggest that the market for motion pictures may have a limited ability to expand during peak seasons. This might be a consequence of capacity constraints or, instead, a consequence of actual moviegoer behavior and a limited market of moviegoers. The implications of the two cases are very different because differing screen allocations would alleviate the former but not the latter. It is questionable whether lost sales in the first weekend should translate into future lost sales. It could be the case that a moviegoer interested in two releases will merely delay the viewing of one of the movies. Krider and Weinberg (1998) findings suggest that the loss is permanent. It is unclear why.

One possible explanation is that moviegoers attend in groups, and it is important that no one in the group has already seen the movie. For motion pictures that have been playing for several weeks, it is likely that one or more members of a group would have already seen the movie (in a different group). In such a case, sales delayed might be sales lost forever. There is no clear evidence, however, that this explanation is sufficient to explain the typical observed promotional pattern of front-loaded promotion.

Second, we must wonder why exhibitors fail to hold movies longer when competition is fierce. Presumably exhibitors fully understand that some purchases are delayed to later periods. Perhaps consumers fail to remember the promotional efforts after several weeks and then fail to see movies that they intended to see in earlier weeks. Perhaps consumers anticipate non-theatrical alternatives. Again, the topic requires further research.

## Endogeneity

Studios, distributors, and exhibitors all make each film decision at different points in time based on available information at that point in time. Hence, one seldom (if ever) sees expected blockbusters being released just before the low season. One seldom (if ever) sees low-budget niche films being released on three thousand screens. Moreover, given that most movies receive some type of preview screening before wide release, advertising budgets tend to be highly correlated with expectations. Hence, movie data have a great potential for endogeneity. Simply, the data lack essential information because certain data points are missing.

One ongoing revisionist wave involves the proper handling of endogeneity caused by the simultaneous decisions of distributors, exhibitors, and consumers. As shown in our preliminary examination of the 2002 launches, ignoring such simultaneity in seasonality can markedly skew results. Elberse and Eliashberg (2003) consider the biases that arise when the launching number of theaters is treated as an exogenous variable rather than as a market outcome that involves the expectations of all players in the sector. Moul (2004b) uses a similar approach to consider the potential biases when incorporating advertising and past admissions, as well as the number of exhibiting theaters. He finds that the primary source of bias arises from mishandling the saturation process, especially when incorporating past admissions. This line of research, of course, is inherently intermediate and serves primarily to answer other questions more accurately.

## SUMMARY

There is now a large and growing literature on the motion picture industry in both marketing and economics. Much is known. For example, we know that early forecasts of motion picture success (i.e., prior to production) are possible and provide some information about the ultimate success of the motion picture. However, unlike packaged goods, considerable variance remains at the pre-production stage. Apparently, there is substantial value added by the director after the filming begins despite elaborate production planning, sophisticated scheduling, and detailed scripts. Of course, it is possible that some unforeseen pre-production variable might greatly enhance pre-production forecasting accuracy.

The situation changes after the film is in the can. At that point, consumer data combined with data on marketing expenditures and data on anticipated screens can create very accurate box-office forecasts. It is important to use the correct consumer data and analyze that data in the proper manner (e.g., Shugan and Swait 2000). After the initial weekend, tracking data can reveal the likely distribution of the box office for a film over time. That data can include new reviews by critics, as well as historical week-to-week box-office data. Data on past seasonal patterns can also be useful for predicting box-office patterns over time.

In general, as Moul (2004a) argues, the process is far from random. Given the appropriate data and the proper models, our ability to predict box office might one day be as good as or exceed the impressive accuracy associated with the prediction of sales for new packaged goods.

### DIRECTIONS FOR NEW RESEARCH

There are three forces that influence theatrical distribution: the consumer, the exhibitor, and competition. The consumer determines demand for the film. That demand depends on many factors, including the date of the release, the extent of the advertising, the positioning of the film, the reputation of the cast, the reputation of the property, the quality of the trailer, critical reviews, as well as word of mouth among consumers. The exhibitor determines the number of screens (based on negotiations with distributors), the time of day the film will show, the ticket price for each screening, and the length of the film's run in the theaters. Other movies compete for the attention of the moviegoer, the limited screens at the theater, and the talent that makes the films (e.g. the cast, the directors).

The existing body of research about these three forces in theatrical distribution, although large, is by no means near completion. There are many important unanswered questions awaiting future research.

For example, why do most movies have such short theatrical runs? It could be that movies are hot when they are released, and movies' brief runs are consumer driven, similar to fashion goods where demand fads can be intense but short lived. An alternative hypothesis is that exhibitors drive theatrical life and drop a film when the demand falls below a particular level. The level might depend on the number of seats occupied in the theater's screening room, as well as the revenue per seat. Still another alternative hypothesis is that distributors determine the theatrical life of the motion picture based on the run time required to support ancillary markets such as VHS sales. Obviously, changes in technology and the growth of giant multi screen theaters might impact all of these factors.

Where and to what extent can marketing influence the profitability of a film? Producers and distributors are very interested in increasing a film's demand after the box office for that film peaks. It is unclear, however, whether marketing can do more than create awareness, shifting sales by getting the same moviegoers to see the film earlier than they would have otherwise. Studios should be very interested in whether market research can predict the demand for a film before a film is made. Even if substantial results are learned, it is unclear whether the creative elements will ever use that market research in their design decisions on the film. Theaters are very interested in selling ancillary services to moviegoers (e.g., popcorn, cappuccinos, arcade services, and so on), but it remains unknown whether marketing has any role in the demand for these ancillary services.

There have been a number of large changes in the environment for distribution in the last decade and their impacts on launching remain uncertain. Has the Web changed the way movies can be launched? New Internet sources are impacting consumer demand by creating new forms of consumer-to-consumer communication, as well as new forms of advertising. Have the structural changes in the exhibition sector changed launching strategies? The multiplex has given exhibitors additional flexibility. Multiple screens allow exhibitors to rapidly adjust the number of screens to meet demand, to keep low-demand films longer by moving them to low-capacity screens, and to show many more competitive films at the same time on different screens at different times. Has this flexibility permanently shifted bargaining power between distributors and exhibitors? Will release strategies change?

Technological advances are impacting the incentives of distributors as well as exhibitors. More revenue is coming from ancillary markets (e.g., DVDs, new pay-per-view technologies, premium satellite channels, sell-through video, and other nontheatrical forms of distribution). These new markets might diminish the importance of the theatrical run because distributors might rush movies to ancillary markets as revenue sources shift. Alternatively, these new markets might increase the importance of the theatrical run because the success in the theatrical run might create the awareness and hype required for success in ancillary markets. More work integrating the theatrical run with ancillary markets is needed.

Changes in ancillary markets might also change the very nature of the movie decision process. Traditionally, movie-choice decisions have been made in groups. Different movies had to compete for the entire group. Once several in a group have seen the film, the likelihood of that group seeing a film diminishes. However, with more films being purchased in after-markets, individuals might change the very nature of their movie-going decision. Individuals might accelerate or postpone seeing individual films based on their expectations of seeing the film in the future through a nontheatrical venue.

The true underlying nature and influence of seasonality requires further investigation. Seasons might merely shift demand from one period to another. Alternatively, seasons might create fleeting periods of opportunity. For a useful thought experiment, suppose exhibitors agreed to show the movie for an entire year (i.e., fifty-two weeks) so that the movie shows in every season. If that film were launched at the start of the peak summer season (say, in early June), would the box office be different than if that film were launched at the end of the summer season (say, in early September)? Moreover, if a film were launched on the same weekend as a very competitive film, would the film still suffer a loss in box office if the theater agreed to carry the film for a longer period of time than when no competitive film was battling for both consumers and screens?

Many questions remain regarding the role of the cast. Obviously, the quality of the acting is important. However, we have yet to determine whether acting is the primary role of a movie star. Other candidates include delivering a guaranteed audience, increasing awareness during the first weekend, producing free publicity through public appearances, drawing other key individuals to the deal (e.g., directors, producers, agents), or enhancing distribution by reassuring exhibitors. Perhaps we should think of stars as substitutes for paid advertising, branding, or a signal of commitment to the film. The question remains wide open.

Should reliable advertising data become available, a movie's theatrical life becomes an opportunity to study the consumer's memory of advertising. How long does the initial advertising blitz last in potential moviegoers' minds? What sort of decay is there from week to week in the effectiveness of a movie's advertising campaign? Do distributors' advertising decisions have an impact beyond movies' theatrical lives – e.g., on rentals and sales in ancillary markets? The concentrated lifespan of movies should allow the analyst to definitively answer such questions, and the answers will have substantial implications for movies and a wide variety of other products.

As is discussed in detail in the next chapter on exhibition, a distributor's launching strategies are made in part within the market between distributors and exhibitors. The price (i.e., rental rate) that clears this market, however, is rarely observed and, consequently, much research on this hidden market has been stymied. Even without additional data on rental rates, however, there is another route to analyzing these relationships. Advances in empirical industrial organization allow the analyst to impose certain assumptions (e.g., distributors maximize weekly profits, exhibitors make their screening decisions based on fixed capacity constraints) and infer what prices would have led to the observed outcomes of theaters in equilibrium. Some recent applications of this method have emphasized the relationship between manufacturers and retailers and consider many of the same issues that would arise in an application to this sector of the motion picture industry. If successful, this sort of analysis could introduce an entirely new literature into movie economics.

As mentioned previously, much of our explanation of theatrical launches has relied on word of mouth. Although obviously important, such an amorphous concept has been notoriously difficult to quantify. This difficulty almost certainly stems from the fact that word of mouth does not have a uniform effect. It hurts the box office for movies that are worse than expected and helps those movies that are better than expected. Additionally, feedback effects (e.g., fewer theaters than expected show a movie with bad word of mouth, a distributor increases advertising for a movie with good word of mouth) compound the measurement challenge. It is only a matter of time, however, before current analytical techniques are able to quantify how well a movie would have performed were it as good as its expectations, and with that quantify word of mouth by contrasting this prediction with what was observed. Such an approach would simultaneously enable us to measure the speed with which information moves among consumers and to consider whether and how well distributors exploit their asymmetric information advantage before release.

Finally, we might apply some of the lessons learned in the motion picture industry to other industries involving similar human value-added components (e.g., creative R&D researchers) and sequential market introductions. These industries might include high-technology component parts, business-related software products, and high-fashion goods.

### REFERENCES

Agresti, Alan, and Larry Winner. 1997. "Evaluating Agreement and Disagreement Among Movie Reviewers," *Chance* 10(2): 10–14.

Ainslie, Andrew, Xavier Drèze, and Fred Zufryden. 2003. "Competition in the Movie Industry," unpublished manuscript, Marketing Department, University of California at Los Angeles Anderson School of Business.

Alba, Joseph, John Lynch, Bart Weitz, Chris Janiszewski, Richard Lutz, Alan Sawyer, and Stacy Wood. 1997. "Interactive Home Shopping: Consumer, Retailer, and Manufacturer Incentives to Participate in Electronic Marketplaces." *Journal of Marketing,* 61(July): 38–53.

Allenby, Greg M., Lichung Jen, and Robert P. Leone. 1996. "Economic Trends and Being Trendy: The Influence of Consumer Confidence on Retail Fashion Sales." *Journal of Business and Economic Statistics,* 14: 103–12.

Austin, Bruce A., and Thomas F. Gordon. 1987. "Movie Genres: Toward a Conceptualized Model and Standardized Definition," *Current Research in Film: Audiences, Economics, and the Law,* Vol. 4, Bruce Austin (ed.). Norwood, NJ: Ablex Publishing Co., 12–33.

Bergen, Mark, Shantanu Dutta, and Steven M. Shugan (1996), "Branded Variants: A Retail Perspective," *Journal of Marketing Research,* 33 (1, February), 9–19.

*BusinessWeek.* 2002. "The Trouble with Tie-Ins; Marketers Are Shying Away from Pricey Hollywood Deals," June 3; Issue 3785: 63.

Chen, Yubo, and Steven Shugan. 2004. "Using New Product Sales to Evaluate Individuals in Teams: Market-Based Metrics and Empirical Evidence from the Entertainment Industry," unpublished manuscript, Marketing Department, University of Florida Warrington School of Business.

Corts, Kenneth S. 2001. "The Strategic Effects of Vertical Market Structure: Common Agency and Divisionalization in the U.S. Motion Picture Industry," *Journal of Economics and Management Strategy*, 10(4): 509–28.

De Vany, Arthur, and Cassey Lee. 2002. "Quality Signals in Information Cascades and the Distribution of Motion Picture Box Office Revenues," *Journal of Economic Dynamics and Control*, 25: 593–694.

De Vany, Arthur, and W. David Walls. 1996. "Bose-Einstein Dynamics and Adaptive Contracting in the Motion Picture Industry," Economic Journal, 106: 1493–514.

De Vany, Arthur, and W. David Walls. 1997. "The Market for Motion Pictures: Rank, Revenue, and Survival," *Economic Inquiry*, 35(4): 783–97.

De Vany, Arthur, and W. David Walls. 1999. "Uncertainty in the Movie Industry: Does Star Power Reduce the Terror of the Box Office?" *Journal of Cultural Economics*, 23(4): 285–318.

Dodds, John C., and Morris B. Holbrook. 1988. "What's an Oscar Worth? An Empirical Estimation of the Effect of Nominations and Awards on Movie Distribution and Revenues," *Current Research in Film: Audiences, Economics, and the Law*, Vol. 4, Bruce Austin (ed.). Norwood, NJ: Ablex Publishing Co.

Dougherty, Philip H. (1983). "Consumers Union Adds Agency to Miller Suit," *The New York Times*, July 22.

Einav, Liran. 2003a. "Gross Seasonality and Underlying Seasonality: Evidence from the U.S. Motion Picture Industry," unpublished manuscript, Economics Department, Stanford University.

———. 2003b. "Not All Rivals Look Alike: Estimating an Equilibrium Model of the Release Date Timing Game," unpublished manuscript, Economics Department, Stanford University.

Elberse, Anita, and Jehoshua Eliashberg. 2003. "Dynamic Behavior of Consumers and Retailers Regarding Sequentially Released Products in International Markets: The Case of Motion Pictures." *Marketing Science*, 22(3): 329–54.

Eliashberg, Jehoshua, J. Jonker, M. Sawhney, and B. Wieranga (2000). "MOVIEMOD: An Implementable Decision Support System for Pre-Release Market Evaluation of Motion Pictures," *Marketing Science*, 19(3): 226–43.

Eliashberg, Jehoshua, and Steven M. Shugan (1997). "Film Critics: Influencers or Predictors?" *Journal of Marketing*, 61: 68–78.

Galloway, Steven. 2003. "Where the Money Went," *Hollywood Reporter*, May 20.

Goettler, Ronald, and Phillip Leslie. 2003. "Co-Financing to Manage Risk in the Motion Picture Industry," unpublished manuscript, Tepper School of Business, Carnegie Mellon University.

Hennig-Thurau, T., G. Walsh, and O. Wruck. 2001. "An Investigation into the Success Factors of Motion Pictures," *Academy of Marketing Science Review*, 1(6).

Hoffman, D., and T. Novak. 1996. "Marketing in Computer-Mediated Environments: Conceptual Foundations," *Journal of Marketing*, 60: 50–68.

Internet Movie DataBase. Retrieved May 2003 from www.imdb.com

Kent, R., and C. Allen. 1994. "Competitive Interference Effects in Consumer Memory for Advertising: The Role of Brand Familiarity," *Journal of Marketing*, 58: 97–105.

Kirmani, A., and A. Rao. 2000. "No Pain, No Gain: A Critical Review of the Literature on Signaling Unobservable Product Quality," *Journal of Marketing*, 64: 66–79.

Kivetz, R., and I. Simonson. 2000. "The Effects of Incomplete Information on Consumer Choice." *Journal of Marketing Research*, 37(4): 427–48.

Knowlton, Steven R. 1998. "Library/Car Sites; Doing the Homework: Reviews of Most Models," *New York Times*, October 1.

Krider, R., and C. Weinberg. 1998. "Competitive Dynamics and the Introduction of New Products: The Motion Picture Timing Game," *Journal of Marketing Research*, 35: 1–15.

Litman, B. 1983. "Predicting Success of Theatrical Movies: An Empirical Study," *Journal of Popular Culture*, 16: 159–75.

Litman, B., and H. Ahn. 1998. "Predicting Financial Success of Motion Pictures," *The Motion Picture Mega-Industry*, B. Litman (ed.). Needham Heights, MA: Allyn & Bacon.

Litman, B., and L. Kohl. 1989. Predicting Financial Success of Motion Pictures: The 80's Experience," *Journal of Media Economics*, 2: 35–50.

Mahajan, Vijay, Eitan Muller, and Frank M. Bass. 1995. "Diffusion of New Products: Empirical Generalizations and Managerial Uses," *Marketing Science; Special Issue on Empirical Generalizations in Marketing*, 14(3): 79–88.

Moul, Charles C. 2001. "Evidence of Qualitative Learning-by-Doing at the Advent of the 'Talkie'," *Journal of Industrial Economics*, 49(1): 97–109.

———. 2004a. "Word of Mouth vs. Market Saturation: Explaining Demand Dynamics for Movies and Music," unpublished manuscript, Economics Department, Washington University (St. Louis).

————. 2004b. "Handling Saturation in Demand: The Case of Motion Pictures," unpublished manuscript, Economics Department, Washington University (St. Louis).

————. 2004c. "Inferring Wholesaler and Retailer Behavior in the Theatrical Distribution of Motion Pictures," unpublished manuscript, Economics Department, Washington University (St. Louis).

Neelamegham, R., and P. Chintagunta. 1999. "A Bayesian Model to Forecast New Product Performance in Domestic and International Markets," *Marketing Science*, 18(2): 115–36.

Pack, Thomas. 1999. "Can You Trust Internet Information?" *Link-up, Medford*, 16, (6) November/December: 24.

Prag, J., and J. Cassavant. 1994. "An Empirical Study of the Determinants of Revenues and Marketing Expenditures in the Motion Picture Industry," *Journal of Cultural Economics*, 18: 217–35.

Radas, S., and S. Shugan. 1998. "Seasonal Marketing and Timing New Product Introductions," *Journal of Marketing Research*. 35(3): 296–315.

Ravid, S. Abraham. 1999. "Information, Blockbusters, and Stars: A Study of the Film Industry," *Journal of Business*, 72(4): 463–92.

Reinstein, David, and Christopher Snyder. 2004. "The Influence of Expert Reviews on Consumer Demand for Experience Goods: A Case Study of Movie Critics," *Journal of Industrial Economics*, forthcoming.

Rust, R., and R. Oliver. 1994. "The Death of Advertising," *Journal of Advertising Research*, 23(4).

Sawhney, M., and J. Eliashberg. 1996. "A Parsimonious Model for Forecasting Gross Box-Office Revenues for Motion Pictures," *Marketing Science*, 15(2): 113–31.

Shugan, Steven M. 1980. "The Cost of Thinking," *Journal of Consumer Research*, 7 (September) 99–111.

Shugan, S., and J. Swait. 2000. "Using Intent Measures to Forecast Motion Picture Success," unpublished manuscript, Marketing Department, University of Florida Warrington School of Business.

Shugan, S., and L. Winner. 2002. "Product Evaluations on the Internet: Marketing Implications," unpublished manuscript, Marketing Department, University of Florida Warrington School of Business.

Smith, S., and V. K. Smith. 1986. "Successful Movies: A Preliminary Empirical Analysis," *Applied Economics*, 18: 501–7.

Swami, S., J. Eliashberg, and C. Weinberg. 1999. "SilverScreener: A Modeling Approach to Movie Screens Management." *Marketing Science*, V. 18(3), 352–72.

Wallace, W. Timothy, Alan Seigerman, and Morris B. Holbrook. 1993. "The Role of Actors and Actresses in the Success of Films: How Much Is a Movie Star Worth?" *Journal of Cultural Economics*, 17(1): 1–27.

Zufryden, Fred. 1996. "Linking Advertising to Box-Office Performance of New Film Releases: A Marketing Planning Model," *Journal of Advertising Research*, July–August, 29–41.

Zufryden, Fred. 2000. "New Film Website Promotion and Box-Office Performance," *Journal of Advertising Research*, January–April, 55–64.

# 5

# The Film Exhibition Business: Critical Issues, Practice, and Research

JEHOSHUA ELIASHBERG

The supply chain for movies released for theatrical exhibition consists of the distributor, exhibitor, and the audience, as shown in Figure 5.1. The audience has opportunities to watch movies in a number of distribution outlets: domestic theaters, foreign theaters, home video, and cable and network TV, where the time lags between the releases of the movies in successive outlets differ but are typically measured in months (Figure 5.2). Despite the availability of these multiple release windows, the theatrical performance of films in the United States has been considered by practitioners to be a critical success driver: "Theatrical exhibition is the major factor in persuading the public what they want to see, even if that public never sets foot inside a motion picture theater. And how well and how long a picture plays in theaters has everything to do with its value in other markets" (Daniels, Leedy, and Sills 1998, p. 34). The main reasons as to why the theatrical experience is believed to have such a significant impact on the performance of the movie in its other distribution channels are the buzz created by the studios prior to and during the theatrical release dates, generated through high advertising spending, and the attention given by the media to box-office performance and figures. It is interesting to note that the recent phenomenon characterized as

**Distributor**     **Exhibitor**     **Audience**

(e.g.,Paramount)     (e.g., Regal Entertainment)

Figure 5.1: Industry structure (the supply chain).

"TV screens get larger and movie theater screens get smaller" has, to date, not had a significant negative impact on the moviegoers' behavior. Watching movies in theater still offers the audience a different experience.

New improvements in theatrical facilities, such as the availability of multiple screens, more comfortable environment, improved sound and picture presentations, and the offering of a range of ancillary products, have led to a sustainable attendance level in the United States, as well as

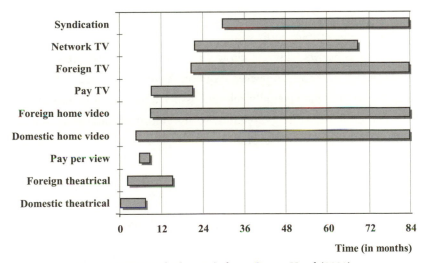

Figure 5.2: Movies' release windows. *Source*: Vogel (2001).

Table 5.1: *Total number of U.S. theaters.*

| Year | Total theaters | 2001 versus | Indoor theaters | 2001 versus | Drive-in theaters | 2001 versus |
|------|----------------|-------------|-----------------|-------------|-------------------|-------------|
| 2001 | 7,070 | – | 6,596 | – | 474 | – |
| 2000 | 7,421 | −4.7% | 6,909 | −4.5% | 512 | −7.4% |
| 1999 | 7,551 | −6.4% | 7,031 | −6.2% | 520 | −8.8% |
| 1998 | 7,418 | −4.7% | 6,894 | −4.3% | 524 | −9.5% |
| 1997 | 7,480 | −5.5% | 6,903 | −4.4% | 577 | −17.9% |
| 1996 | 7,798 | −9.3% | 7,215 | −8.6% | 583 | −18.7% |
| 1995 | 7,744 | −8.7% | 7,151 | −7.8% | 593 | −20.1% |

*Source:* MPAA Worldwide Market Research.

in large foreign markets such as the United Kingdom (Doyle 1998) and even in smaller countries such as Thailand (Towira 2000).

In this chapter, I focus on the first two theatrical release windows: domestic and foreign theaters. The chapter is organized as follows. I first review the reality of the theatrical exhibition business today, offering observations as well as conjectures concerning its future. The proposed hypotheses can be viewed as opportunities for formal research. Some of them have already received research attention – others have not. I provide a representative survey of the extant literature. The range of methodologies employed to study the various issues is quite broad. It covers econometrics, discrete-choice, and operations research models. My focus in this chapter, however, is not on the methodologies employed but, instead, on managerially relevant issues and questions examined and on their key findings. I conclude with a summary and discussion of opportunities for further research.

## IS THE U.S. MARKET (STILL) OVER-SCREENED?

The U.S. theatrical distribution consists of theater chains (circuits) and independent exhibitors. Table 5.1 shows the evolution of the total number of U.S. theaters operating in 2001 and Table 5.2 depicts the

Table 5.2: *Total number of U.S. screens.*

| Year | Total screens | 2001 versus | Indoor screens | 2001 versus | Drive-in screens | 2001 versus |
|------|------|------|------|------|------|------|
| 2001 | 36,764 | – | 36,110 | – | 654 | – |
| 2000 | 37,396 | −1.7% | 36,679 | −1.6% | 717 | −8.8% |
| 1999 | 37,185 | −1.1% | 36,448 | −0.9% | 737 | −11.3% |
| 1998 | 34,186 | 7.5% | 33,440 | 8.0% | 746 | −12.3% |
| 1997 | 31,640 | 16.2% | 30,825 | 17.1% | 815 | −19.8% |
| 1996 | 29,690 | 23.8% | 28,864 | 25.1% | 826 | −20.8% |
| 1995 | 27,805 | 32.2% | 26,958 | 33.9% | 847 | −22.8% |
| 1990 | 23,689 | 55.2% | 22,774 | 58.6% | 915 | −28.5% |
| 1985 | 21,147 | 73.8% | 18,327 | 97.0% | 2,820 | −76.8% |
| 1980 | 17,590 | 109.0% | 14,029 | 157.4% | 3,561 | −81.6% |

*Source:* MPAA Worldwide Market Research.

dynamics of the total number of screens available to the public. Jointly, the two tables suggest that the year 2000 may be considered as a turning point, the year when the exhibition industry started a trend of downward adjustment of the total number of screens available in the U.S. The growth rates in the total number of screens between 1997 and 1998 (8 percent) and between 1998 and 1999 (9 percent), for example, are higher than the corresponding growth rates in the number of admissions (6.5 percent and −0.6 percent, respectively). This gap may have been one factor that led the industry to conclude that the U.S. market is over-screened. Although the total number of screens rose from 22,921 in 1989 to 37,185 in 1999 (62 percent growth rate), the number of admissions has shown a lower growth rate of only 17 percent (from 1.26 billion to 1.47 billion). The fact that the United States is over-screened is also suggested by comparative cross-country statistics. For example, considering screens per 1 million people, the United States is ranked first, followed by France, Germany, Italy, and the United Kingdom (Figure 5.3). In the United Kingdom, for instance, the annual growth of cinema screens has been more moderate compared with the United States (see Table 5.3).

Table 5.3: *The UK motion picture industry (1995–2002)*

|  | 1995 | 1996 | 1997 | 1998 | 1999 | 2000 | 2001 | 2002 |
|---|---|---|---|---|---|---|---|---|
| Admissions (million) | 115 | 124 | 139 | 136 | 140 | 143 | 156 | 176 |
| Cinema sites | 743 | 742 | 747 | 759 | 692 | 686 | 692 | 668 |
| Cinema screens | 2,019 | 2,166 | 2,383 | 2,564 | 2,758 | 2,954 | 3,614 | 3,258 |
| Multiplex sites | 79 | 95 | 142 | 167 | 186 | 209 | 224 | 222 |
| Multiplex screens | 706 | 859 | 1,222 | 1,488 | 1,727 | 2,003 | 2,170 | 2,215 |
| Average ticket price (£) | 3.43 | 2.81 | 3.68 | 3.83 | 3.80 | 4.00 | 4.14 | 4.29 |
| Box office gross (£M) | 384 | 426 | 506 | 515 | 571 | 577 | 652 | 755 |

*Source:* British Film Institute (2004).

Davis (2003b), however, claims that distinguishing between first-run and second-run theaters shows that the growth in domestic first-run screens has been far less than what is implied by the raw gross screen count. He examines a panel data set documenting the extent and nature of exit, entry, and revenue cannibalization that occurred during the 1990s in the U.S. exhibition sector. Although an exact answer to the question of social over-screening requires as-yet uncalculated measures of consumer surplus and cost, this study indicates that a substantial portion of a new theater's demand is "stolen" from existing theaters rather than composed

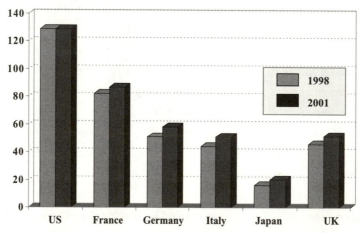

Figure 5.3: Screens per 1 million people. *Source*: EAO (2002).

of new consumers. Because such business stealing is a necessary condition for the over-screening argument, the question remains open. He is able, however, to use Canadian theater data to argue that the sector is over-screened from an industry profit-maximizing viewpoint.

## THE MARKET WILL BECOME MORE CONCENTRATED: MORE EXPANSION AND HORIZONTAL INTEGRATIONS (MERGERS AND ACQUISITIONS) ARE LIKELY TO OCCUR, AND THE PLAYERS WILL BE DIFFERENT

The exhibition industry has been undergoing major structural changes recently. Two snapshots of the industry demonstrate those changes. As of May 1, 1994, the exhibition chains United Artist Theaters, Carmike Cinemas, Cineplex Odeon, AMC Entertainment, and General Cinema Theaters owned a total of 8,473 screens, which amounted then to 33 percent of the total U.S. screens. By comparison, in the United Kingdom, in 1998 the leading five exhibitors (for example, Odeon, UCI, and Virgin Cinemas) accounted for more than 60 percent of the total screens. Given this discrepancy, it is not surprising that concentration in the U.S. exhibition market has risen in recent years. This prognosis, however, might be questioned by those who note the fairly stable number of films released in the United States annually by the studios (Figure 5.4). It is conceivable that more movies may have been produced and were looking for exhibition opportunities, but the exceedingly high average print and advertising expenditures necessary to support their theatrical distribution ($31 million on average in 2002) prohibit the distributors from releasing them. In such a case, the supply of movies has been less than the "shelf-space" available to play them.

At present, the U.S. exhibition landscape looks quite different from 1994. The top five exhibition chains in 2003 were Regal Entertainment Group with 5,850 screens in 552 sites, AMC Entertainment with 3,308 screens in 235 sites, Carmike Cinema with 2,333 screens in 323 sites,

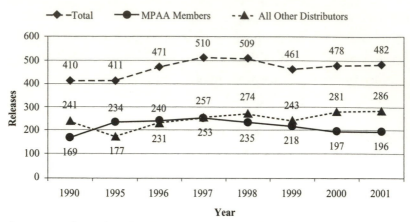

Figure 5.4: Films released in the United States. *Source*: MPAA Workwide Market Research.

Cinemark USA with 2,241 screens in 191 sites, and Loews Cineplex Entertainment with 2,161 screens in 226 sites. They accounted for 44.6 percent of the total number of screens and 25 percent of the total number of sites. (Note that seats per screen have declined over time.) In fact, just recently, Regal Entertainment announced that it would purchase half of Hoyts Cinemas' U.S. theaters (fifty-two of Hoyts' ninety-two theaters), thus extending its reach into the Northeast market. Regal Entertainment, under the leadership of Philip Anschuts, will expand its reach to 6,100 screens by next year. The Denver-based company reported that 2002 "was a block-buster year for Regal" (Diorio 2003). Annual revenue climbed 13 percent to $2.27 billion.

Niche players will also play an increasingly important role in the industry in the future. For example, GameWorks, a Los Angeles–based chain of arcade/restaurants, has announced a $20 million project in Oklahoma City to build a multiplex with "GameWorks elements" including games, a restaurant, bars, and bowling (Emmons 2001). Muvico Theaters, a Florida-based exhibitor founded in 1984, now owns 104 screens. It pursues an expansion strategy "to develop, acquire and operate state-of-the-art megaplex theaters in entertainment centers in mid-sized metropolitan markets and suburban growth areas of larger metropolitan markets in any suitable location." Indeed, exhibition circuits tend to operate in certain regions as local monopolists and sometime duopolists (for instance, Carmike operates in small cities where it faces little competition). In Birmingham, Alabama, for example, the theater exhibition is almost evenly divided between two chains: Regal Cinemas with fifty-two screens and Carmike with forty-eight screens, "resulting in moviegoers being offered a very limited range of films, forcing adventurous viewers to travel to other cities or wait half a year for video releases" (Brasell 1999).

Since the mandated separation of distribution and exhibition in 1948, integration in the exhibition sector has been horizontal rather than vertical.[1] Horizontal integration has occurred through new real estate selection and development as well as mergers and acquisitions. Market expansion via new sites selection is one of exhibitors' key strategic decisions. The local population is typically the most important factor. The age demographics and, to some extent, economics of local consumers play the substantial roles. A rule of thumb employed by some practicing executives is one screen for every ten thousand people with estimated attendance of 5.5 movies per year per person. Based on such a heuristics and assuming an even exogenous arrival distribution (ten thousand moviegoers per 2.182 months) and thirty-six key showings per month (4 weekends × 3 days per weekend × 3 showings per day), the seating capacity needed to accommodate the audience is 127 seats per screening room $(10,000/(2.182 \times 36))$.

Cross-sectional demand results in Davis (2001) suggest that consumers are generally unwilling to travel and, consequently, theaters may be close to local monopolies. Given this market power, local markets may underprovide movie screens relative to the socially optimal number.

---

[1] In that year, a suit that was previously filed by the U.S. Department of Justice concluded with the "Paramount decrees," which prohibited the distributors from vertical integration. Since the 1980s, however, the regulation has been relaxed by allowing a number of distributors (e.g., Sony, Paramount, and Warner Brothers) to have exhibition interests as long as their percentage of the total number of screens remains low.

Davis (2003a) uses the same data to examine the issue of price differentiation across geographic markets, as well as the relationship between local competition and admission prices. He finds that "the effect of the presence of local competition on adult admission prices, though often highly statistically significant, is economically relatively small unless the theaters are very close to one another" (p. 23). Hence, concerns regarding a possible rise in admission prices as a result of the recent mergers and acquisitions wave are not supported by his analysis. Although these papers each make useful methodological contributions, their conclusions contradict those of Davis (2003b), where business-stealing is common. This difference probably arises from the use of cross-sectional data in Davis (2001, 2003a) and panel data in Davis (2003b). Given the additional variation typically associated with panel data, the results of Davis (2003b) are likely more credible.

## THE CONTRACTUAL ARRANGEMENT BETWEEN THE DISTRIBUTOR AND THE EXHIBITOR WILL CHANGE

The decision to negotiate directly with theaters or to solicit bids is a business judgment made by the distributor. Most contractual arrangements between the distributor and the exhibitor stipulate a minimum playing time and an agreement as to how the box-office receipts are to be shared between the two parties. For many major movies, a sliding-scale agreement is used. Exhibitors pay the largest of the amounts implied by the three following possibilities. The primary term is the rental rate, setting what percentage of total admissions receipts the exhibitor will cede to the distributor. These rental rates vary across movies, across theaters, and across weeks for a given movie at a given theater. Rates typically fall from 60 or 70 percent in a movie's opening week to 30 percent in the movie's final weeks, but substantial deviations from this baseline are common.

Contracts have two additional components: (1) an after-house allowance ("nut") split (usually 90 percent to the distributor), and (2) a floor. The nut is based on theater capacity and is recognition, on the distributor's part, that the exhibitor incurs expenses in running the facility (for example, rent, insurance, maintenance). The floor serves as a guaranteed minimum for the distributor. Of course, the specific values of the split, floor, and rental rate are determined by the relative power of the two parties. The key power bases are the relative shortage (surplus) of screens, the total number of screens the exhibitor owns, and the potential success of the movie to be shown. Whereas the exhibitor's share of the ticket sales increases as the movie is playing for a longer period of time, the downside is that the distributor normally stops the advertising/promotion support after the first two or three weeks of the movie's run. This gives rise to two options the exhibitor faces: obtaining a small share from a large pie (playing a newly released movie) or a large share from a smaller pie (playing an ongoing movie longer).

Although legally the determination of the admission price is in the hands of the exhibitor, the distributor monitors it informally. The admission price raises a contracting problem: the exhibitor might prefer a lower price in order to compete more effectively with other exhibitors. Lower ticket prices may also increase attendance and, consequently, the revenues from concessions, a revenue source not shared with the distributor. The distributor, however, would prefer a higher ticket price (Caves 2000). Several years ago, Edgar Bronfman, then CEO of Universal, put forward an innovative but controversial ticket-pricing idea (Battaglio and Honeycutt 1998). He suggested that admission prices of movies be differentiated on bases such as production budget and star power. Moreover, Bronfman argued that the demand for movies in their opening weekend is inelastic and, hence, there may be room for temporal price discrimination. Such pricing schemes can increase the size of the pie that the distributor/exhibitor share, thereby making both parties better off. The industry has not adopted similar price-discrimination ideas for reasons such as the absence of an agreed-upon base for across-titles pricing and the lack of coordination among exhibitors in terms of temporal price discrimination.

Research questions related to the issues mentioned herein include a reexamination of the current contract in terms of its timeliness and fairness and the uniformity of movie ticket prices across titles and over time. The first issue, reexamination of the contractual arrangement, raises the possibility that, until the exhibition sector sufficiently reduces capacity, implicit block-booking arrangement of films is quite likely to prevail. Block-booking involves selling motion pictures as a package. It was banned by the U.S. Supreme Court in 1962 on grounds that the practice was unfair to the exhibitor because it forced them to play movies that *ex post* turned out to be unsuccessful.[2] Arguing against the ruling, Stigler (1968) pointed out the potentially welfare-enhancing aspects of the practice. Furthermore, in a recent study, Hanssen (2002) argues that the block-booking arrangement was not an unfair practice but instead a necessity that provided product.

The question of uniform prices across titles (successful and unsuccessful) and over time has received some attention by Einav and Orbach (2001). They identified flaws in this pricing policy and provided explanations and possible justifications for the uniform prices. The justifications include perceived price unfairness by consumers, movies' short life cycle that limits the exhibitors' opportunity to adjust prices once the uncertainty concerning the popularity of the movie is resolved, diverging exhibitors and distributors interests, and the instability of the demand.

## CONSUMERS WILL BECOME MORE LOYAL TO THEATER CIRCUITS AND SITES

Consumers follow different decision-making processes in selecting what movie to watch, at what time during the day, and in what theater. Based on anecdotal evidence, one may distinguish between two behavioral processes: (1) movie first–theater next, or (2) theater first–movie next.

---

[2] United States v. Loew's Inc., 371 U.S. 38 (1962).

Under the former process, which is more common in the United States, the consumer first decides on the movie and then selects the most convenient site. Under the latter process, more commonly observed in foreign markets, the consumer first attends his or her favorite theater and, once there, decides on the movie.

Theater circuits in the United States are trying to induce more consumers to adopt the theater first–movie next heuristic. AMC Entertainment, for example, has a program called "MovieWatcher," which provides moviegoers various benefits including free tickets, concessions, and entertainment news. This program, which is very similar to that of other service providers such as airlines and hotels, has been designed to create loyalty to a particular theater circuit and, possibly, to a particular site. It requires proper marketing and advertising efforts by exhibitors, as well as other perks such as "after-movie mints . . . and ushers who even clean the snow from windshields" to ensure that the loyalty to the theater is retained (Eller 2002). In a more rigorous work, Davis (2001) develops an econometric model of movie demand, considering theater characteristics (price and quality), as well as the distances consumers have to travel. He finds statistically significant preferences for theaters with digital projection, THX sound, and more screens. He also offers estimates of relative magnitudes. THX sound and digital projection have approximately the same effect on consumer decisions, and adding about seven additional screens generates the same effect on demand as introducing THX or digital.

### THE DIGITAL TECHNOLOGY: THREATS AND OPPORTUNITIES

Technological advances in new digital technologies are likely to present threats as well as opportunities to the exhibition industry. (Chapter 2 detailed the likely benefits of digital technologies to production.) New peer-to-peer networks make sharing large electronic files such as movies faster and easier. Distribution via the Internet may affect movie-going behavior. "By the end of the year it is estimated that one million

Table 5.4: *(Illegal) distribution via the Internet: How widespread is it?*

| Media Force's Top 10 Pirated Movies List (August 2001) | |
|---|---|
| Title | Distributor |
| 1. American Pie | Universal |
| 2. The Fast and the Furious | Universal |
| 3. Shrek | DreamWorks |
| 4. Jurassic Park III | Universal |
| 5. The Matrix | Warner Bros |
| 6. Planet of the Apes | 20th Century Fox |
| 7. Crouching Tiger, Hidden Dragon | Sony |
| 8. Swordfish | Warner Bros |
| 9. Traffic | USA Films |
| 10. Fight Club | 20th Century Fox |

*Source:* Media Force (October 2001).

illegal downloads will take place every day," said Jack Valenti (MPAA press release, April 3, 2001). Table 5.4 shows the titles of the most pirated movies in 2001. It appears that the piracy increases the buzz, but at the same time leads to losses in ticket and video sales. Distributors and studios are attempting to fight the piracy threat via simultaneous release of movies in the U.S. and foreign markets, court battles, and by educating and inducing consumers to use legal Internet distributions, such as the networks established by the studios and distributors themselves (for example, Movielink.com). Movie exhibitors, on the other hand, believe that it is unlikely that the experience of watching a movie on a computer screen will cannibalize the theatrical experience and, hence, they remain largely unconcerned with the piracy threat.

Digital cinema, which is a means of projecting a moving image without using a reel of film, is another technology on the horizon that will have impacts on several sectors of the movie business, exhibition in particular (Table 5.5). Its superiority lies in both its image and sound quality and its lack of deterioration with time and multiple showings. Its projected

Table 5.5: *Digital cinemas: How widespread are they?*

---

- July 1999: Disney announces that "Tarzan," the studio's latest animation feature, will be screened electronically using Texas Instruments prototype projectors in three theatrical venues.
- February 2000: Texas Instruments brings its DLP Cinema technology to Europe, with screenings of "Toy Story 2" in Paris, Brussels, London, and Manchester, in cooperation with Technicolor's Real Image Digital.
- November 2000: Disney division Miramax premieres "Bounce" digitally in New York with satellite delivery courtesy of Boeing. Other partners are Texas Instruments, QuVis, and AMC Theaters. Miramax had previously screened "Shakespeare in Love" and "Life Is Beautiful" using JVC's ILA e-cinema technology.
- January 2001: National Cinema Network (NCN) debuts its Digital Theatre Distribution System (DTDS) for e-cinema advertising on 83 screens in three U.S. theaters in Anaheim (CA), Kansas City (MO), and New York (NY).

---

*Source:* Screen Digest (2001).

market penetration is debatable:

> A survey conducted as part of the Celluloid of Silicon initiative reports that "a clear majority of respondents think that at least 40 percent of European screens will be digital by 2010."
>
> (*Screen Digest Report* 2002, p. 43)

> By 2006 we do not expect more than 1,000 screens, or less than 3% of the country's 35,700 screens, to be digitally capable.
>
> (PricewaterhouseCoopers 2002)

> Although progress has been made in some areas . . . , it has not been made in economics. . . . With economics likely to remain a challenge, we pushed back our original 5% penetration estimate for digital cinema screen from 2004 to 2006.
>
> (Credit Suisse First Boston, 2002)

Its likely impact is more certain. Digital cinema will reduce the print and advertising cost of a movie to the distributor and studio, but it will require the exhibitor to invest heavily in digital projectors

($100,000–$150,000 per screen) and other infrastructure (for example, data storage and satellite dishes), as well as in operational and service support. If digital projection devices are adopted, they will almost certainly increase the exhibitor's house allowance in the contract but simultaneously increase the distributor's control over how the exhibitor manages the allocation of movies to screens. It will also offer a number of new opportunities: (1) higher ticket prices from offering an enhanced consumer experience; (2) alternative and flexible programming opportunities such as screening live events (for example, sports, concerts), games and interactive films, and business conferences; and (3) new advertising possibilities, probably tailored to local audiences. Regal Entertainment Group has already introduced a 20-minute "preshow" loaded with ads before every film at its twenty-seven Philadelphia-area theaters (Hiltbrand 2003).

### EXHIBITION EXECUTIVES FACE A COMPLEX STRATEGIC SPACE

In the near future, the strategic agenda of the top management of an exhibition circuit will consist of the following decisions: new sites selection, lease negotiation, facility design, hiring and training personnel, theater marketing and pricing, capacity management via other business models, and, of course, film procurement and film scheduling (macro and micro) in the facility. The research already conducted in this area can be classified as taking one of two perspectives: the industry's or an individual exhibitor's, discussed herein.

Film procurement is a multidimensional decision. It involves considerations such as what type of movies ratings (for example, G, PG, PG-13, R, NC-17, NR) to play in the theaters in order to maintain competitive positioning appealing to the local audience and how far in advance to book the selected movies. The exhibitor's procurement strategy provides the basis for a macroscheduling plan; allocating the movies to different screens can then be managed adaptively as actual demand reveals itself.

To consider the first of these dimensions, Leenders and Eliashberg (2004) examined the commercial performance of locally rated movies in terms of their parental guidance in different countries. Taking an industry rather than a particular exhibitor's perspective, they considered the fact that the same movie often obtains different ratings in different countries. For example, the movie *Godzilla* was rated PG-13 in the United States, PG in Australia, and suitable for eleven years or older in Sweden. They analyzed the commercial performance of movies released by major studios in the United States in 1997 and 1998 and in foreign countries such as the United Kingdom, France, Germany, Sweden, Spain, and Italy. They found not only that the effect of a restrictive movie rating on commercial performance outside the United States may be less severe (that is, less negative), but also that it may even have a positive impact in more masculine countries (for example, Italy). For forecasting box-office tickets sales, see Sawhney and Eliashberg (1996).

Jones and Ritz (1991), interested in the exhibitors' adaptive behavior, have also taken an industry's perspective in their modeling of the interaction between demand for movies and shelf-space supply of screens. Their model incorporates the dynamic behavior of the "average" consumer and exhibitor, and it provides an analytical basis for the temporal behavior of movies and their corresponding screens. Another industry-level analysis has been conducted by Elberse and Eliashberg (2003). They study the extent to which exhibitors respond adaptively to the demand for movies in the United States as well as in foreign markets. Their empirical analyses reveal that variables such as movie attributes and advertising expenditures, which are typically assumed to influence audiences directly, mostly do so *indirectly* through their impact on exhibitors' screen allocations. They also found that the longer is the time lag between releases, the weaker is the relationship between the U.S. and foreign market performance – an effect that is mostly driven by exhibitors' screen allocations. Swami, Puterman,

Table 5.6: *Data: Restricted consideration set (list of movies played at the theater on all six screens).*

| | |
|---|---|
| 1. *The Accused* (TA) | 23. *Major League* (ML) |
| 2. *Batman* (B) | 24. *Miss Firecracker* (MF) |
| 3. *Chances Are* (CA) | 25. *New York Stories* (NYS) |
| 4. *Cookie* (C) | 26. *Night Game* (NG) |
| 5. *Dangerous Liaisons* (DL) | 27. *A Nightmare on Elm Street V* (NESS) |
| 6. *Dead-Bang* (DB) | 28. *No Holds Barred* (NHB) |
| 7. *Dead Calm* (DC) | 29. *The Package* (TP) |
| 8. *Dead Poets Society* (DPS) | 30. *Pet Sematary* (PS) |
| 9. *Disorganized Crime* (DC) | 31. *Peter Pan* (PP) |
| 10. *Earth Girls Are Easy* (EGE) | 32. *Pink Cadillac* (PC) |
| 11. *For Queen and Country* (FQC) | 33. *Police Academy 6* (PA6) |
| 12. *Friday the 13th, Part VIII* (FT8) | 34. *Relentless* (RL) |
| 13. *Heathers* (H) | 35. *Rude Awakening* (RA) |
| 14. *Honey, I Shrunk the Kids* (HISK) | 36. *Scandal* (SDL) |
| 15. *Indiana Jones and the Last Crusade* (U) | 37. *See No Evil, Hear No Evil* (SNEHNE) |
| 16. *Lean On Me* (LOM) | 38. *See You in The Morning* (SYM) |
| 17. *Lethal Weapon 2* (LW2) | 39. *Sing* (SING) |
| 18. *Let It Ride* (LIR) | 40. *Speed Zone* (SZ) |
| 19. *Leviathan* (LTHN) | 41. *Star Trek V: The Final Frontier* (ST5) |
| 20. *License To Kill* (LTK) | 42. *Turner and Hooch* (TH) |
| 21. *Lock Up* (LU) | 43. *UHF* |
| 22. *Lover Boy* (LB) | |

and Weinberg (2001) have demonstrated how an exhibitor's movie replacement problem under stochastic environment can be modeled as a Markovian decision process where the decision maker observes the system state and chooses a course of action. Their analyses show that two practical heuristics, presumably employed by some exhibitors, are markedly outperformed by the optimal policy.

Work related to macroscheduling of an individual exhibitor is exemplified in Swami, Eliashberg, and Weinberg (1999). They conducted an *ex post* analysis for a six-screen theater located in New York. In that analysis, the facility's profitability for movies playing in 1989, over a twenty-seven week period, was analyzed based on publicly available data and

| Week \ Screen | 1 | 2 | 3 | 4 | 5 | 6 |
|---|---|---|---|---|---|---|
| 1 | NYS | CA | DL | LOM | PA6 | LTHN |
| 2 | NYS | CA | DL | LOM | DB | LTHN |
| 3 | DL | NYS | CA | H | DB | SING |
| 4 | DL | NYS | ML | H | DC | TA |
| 5 | DOC | ML | NYS | H | DC | TA |
| 6 | SYM | ML | DOC | PS | SZ | H |
| 7 | SYM | LB | ML | SDL | PS | H |
| 8 | SYM | LB | ML | SDL | PS | MF |
| 9 | SNEHNE | EGE | ML | SDL | PS | MF |
| 10 | SNEHNE | EGE | FOC | SDL | PS | MF |
| 11 | EGE | PC | IJ | IJ | SDL | SNEHNE |
| 12 | DPS | NHB | IJ | IJ | SNEHNE | PC |
| 13 | DPS | ST5 | ST5 | IJ | IJ | SNEHNE |
| 14 | DPS | ST5 | ST5 | IJ | IJ | SNEHNE |
| 15 | IJ | ST5 | DPS | B | B | HISK |
| 16 | IJ | ST5 | DPS | B | B | HISK |
| 17 | IJ | LW2 | DPS | B | B | HISK |
| 18 | LTK | LW2 | B | IJ | PP | HISK |
| 19 | LTK | LW2 | B | IJ | UHF | HISK |
| 20 | LTK | LW2 | B | TH | FT8 | HISK |
| 21 | LTK | LW2 | B | TH | FT8 | LU |
| 22 | LTK | LU | B | TH | FT8 | NES5 |
| 23 | RA | LR | B | LU | LW2 | NES5 |
| 24 | LR | TP | B | LU | LW2 | C |
| 25 | DPS | TP | B | RL | LW2 | C |
| 26 | DPS | TP | B | RL | LW2 | C |
| 27 | RL | TP | B | C | LW2 | NG |

Figure 5.5: Actual schedule of movies at a NYC theater.

under several assumptions concerning house allowance, sliding shares, and concession profits (see Table 5.6 and Figure 5.5 for the actual set of movies the theater chose to play during the time period of interest). The set of movies actually selected by the theater for running is called the *restricted* considerations set. An integer programming-based model (SILVERSCREENER) has been developed and applied to assess the potential for profitability improvement. Figure 5.6 shows the optimal schedule the model recommended. The optimality (net contribution from tickets and concession sales) is taken from the exhibitor's perspective and it considers explicitly the fact that the longer the movie is playing, the larger is the exhibitor's share of the box-office grosses. (The movie NYS [*New York Stories*], for instance, actually played for five weeks whereas the model

| Week \ Screen | 1 | 2 | 3 | 4 | 5 | 6 |
|---|---|---|---|---|---|---|
| 1 | NYS | CA | DL | LOM | PA6 | LTHN |
| 2 | NYS | CA | DL | LOM | DB | LTHN |
| 3 | NYS | H | DL | LOM | DB | LTHN |
| 4 | NYS | H | TA | LOM | DC | ML |
| 5 | NYS | H | TA | LOM | DC | ML |
| 6 | NYS | H | TA | LOM | PS | ML |
| 7 | NYS | H | MF | SDL | PS | ML |
| 8 | NYS | H | MF | SDL | PS | ML |
| 9 | NYS | H | MF | SDL | SYM | SNEHNE |
| 10 | NYS | H | EGE | SDL | SYM | SNEHNE |
| 11 | IJ | H | EGE | SDL | IJ | SNEHNE |
| 12 | IJ | H | EGE | DPS | IJ | SNEHNE |
| 13 | IJ | ST5 | EGE | DPS | IJ | ST5 |
| 14 | IJ | ST5 | EGE | DPS | IJ | ST5 |
| 15 | IJ | HISK | B | DPS | IJ | B |
| 16 | IJ | HISK | B | DPS | IJ | B |
| 17 | LW2 | HISK | B | DPS | IJ | B |
| 18 | LW2 | LTK | B | DPS | IJ | B |
| 19 | LW2 | LTK | B | DPS | IJ | B |
| 20 | LW2 | LTK | B | DPS | TH | B |
| 21 | LW2 | LTK | B | DPS | TH | B |
| 22 | LW2 | NES5 | B | DPS | TH | B |
| 23 | LW2 | NES5 | B | DPS | TH | B |
| 24 | LW2 | C | TP | DPS | TH | B |
| 25 | LW2 | C | TP | DPS | TH | B |
| 26 | LW2 | LU | TP | DPS | TH | B |
| 27 | LW2 | LU | TP | DPS | TH | B |

Figure 5.6: Optimal schedule generated by SCREENER-I (ex-post) (for the restricted consideration case).

recommended it should have played for ten weeks.) Clearly, there was money left on the table. The exhibitor could have increased the theater's profitability by 38 percent by running fewer movies for a longer period of time (Table 5.7). The tendency to actually play more movies for a shorter time period may be explained by the pressure the distributors put on the exhibitor. The room for profitability improvement gets even larger when the exhibitor is allowed to procure movies from a larger (*expanded*) set of movies running elsewhere in the country over the same twenty-seven week period (Table 5.8). In that case, the profitability could have gone up by 121 percent (Table 5.9). The SilverScreener model has been implemented by an exhibition circuit in Europe, first for a single facility and

Table 5.7: *Potential for improving cumulative profit to the exhibitor: "Money left on the table" for the restricted set case.*

| | |
|---|---|
| Estimated actual profit: | $585,175 |
| Number of different movies: | 43 |
| Estimated profit (restricted set): | $805,988 |
| Number of different movies: | 27 |
| Profitability improvement: | 38% |

Table 5.8: *Expanded consideration set (movies played at NYC theater and other movies played elsewhere during the same period).*

| | |
|---|---|
| 44. *The Abyss* (TAB) | 66. *Miracle Mile* (MM) |
| 45. *Adventures of Baron Munchausen* (ABM) | 67. *Parenthood* (PH) |
| 46. *Adventures of Milo & Otis* (AMO) | 68. *Rain Man* (RM) |
| 47. *Bill and Ted's Excellent Adventure* (BTA) | 69. *Red Scorpion* (RS) |
| 48. *Casualties of War* (COW) | 70. *Renegades* (RG) |
| 49. *Cheetah* (CH) | 71. *The Rescuers* (TR) |
| 50. *Cousins* (CSN) | 72. *Road House* (RH) |
| 51. *Criminal Law* (CL) | 73. *Rood Tops* (RT) |
| 52. *Cyborg* (CBRG) | 74. *Say Anything* (SA) |
| 53. *The Dream Team* (TDT) | 75. *Sea of Love* (SOL) |
| 54. *Do the Right Thing* (DRT) | 76. *Sex, Lies and Videotape* (SLV) |
| 55. *Field of Dreams* (FD) | 77. *Shag* (SHAG) |
| 56. *Fletch Lives* (FL) | 78. *She's Out of Control* (SOC) |
| 57. *Ghostbusters II* (GB2) | 79. *Skin Deep* (SD) |
| 58. *Great Balls of Fire* (GBOF) | 80. *Troop Beverly Hills* (TBH) |
| 59. *The Horror Show* (THS) | 81. *Uncle Buck* (UB) |
| 60. *How I Got into College* (HGC) | 82. *Weekend at Bernie's* (WB) |
| 61. *K-9* | 83. *When Harry Met Sally* (WHMS) |
| 62. *The Karate Kid III* (KK3) | 84. *Winter People* (WP) |
| 63. *Kick Boxer* (KB) | 85. *Wired* (WIRED) |
| 64. *Listen to Me* (LTM) | 86. *Working Girl* (WG) |
| 65. *Lost Angels* (LA) | 87. *Young Einstein* (YE) |

Table 5.9: *Potential for improving cumulative*
*profit to the exhibitor: "Money left on the table"*
*for the expanded set case*

| | |
|---|---|
| Estimated actual profit: | $585,175 |
| Number of different movies: | 43 |
| Estimated profit (expanded set) | $1,294,408 |
| Number of different movies: | 25 |
| Profitability improvement: | 121% |

later for multiple facilities, each having multiple screens, in the same city (Eliashberg, Swami, Weinberg, and Wierenga, 2001). The results indicate actual improvement in the exhibitor's profitability compared to a control group.

Situations where the analysis takes the viewpoint of the movie's exhibitor and its distributor simultaneously have also been studied. Such a situation is described in Eliashberg, Jonker, Sawhney, and Wierenga (2000). A pre-release forecasting and diagnostic decision support system, MOVIEMOD, has been developed and implemented in Europe. The implementation evaluated media (advertising) and distribution (weekly screens allocation) plans for the movie *Shadow Conspiracy* and led to modification of the plans and, consequently, to an improved performance.

## SUMMARY AND OPPORTUNITIES FOR FURTHER RESEARCH

It is encouraging to observe that some research has been conducted with respect to various critical exhibition-business–related issues. This research has already made some and is likely to make even more of an impact in the future of the exhibition business. However, there still remain a number of open questions that provide opportunities for further research.

I am not aware of any rigorous research that takes an industry perspective and addresses the important questions: What is the nature of the power structure in the industry? How has it changed over time? What are its key determinants? What role will art houses play in the future? What differences, if any, should be included in contracts signed with art-house exhibitors?

The contracting terms of producers, actors, and other members of the creative community have already received some research attention via the principal–agent framework (Chisholm 1997) and other frameworks (Weinstein 1998). Surprisingly, however, not much has been done with respect to the exhibitor–distributor contractual relationship. This also represents a promising area for further research.

The digitalization phenomenon offers a number of interesting opportunities for research, including identifying potential pirates of intellectual properties such as movies; understanding their motivation; analyzing consumers with respect to the extent to which they notice, appreciate, and are willing to pay for the incremental benefits of a digital versus analogue entertainment experience; and predicting and controlling the diffusion of digital exhibition. With regard to the first two questions, research related to the personality characteristics (Wagner and Sanders 2001) and the national culture (Husted 2000) of software pirates might be helpful. Other open questions concerning the digital projection include: How will it change the distributor–exhibitor relationship? The contractual arrangement? What theater size and other economies of scale justify the investment in the infrastructure? How will it affect the exhibitor's control over screens allocation? Operational efficiency?

Is there room for additional profitability improvement by microscheduling the movies already selected for the theater? The microscheduling problem involves modeling the performance of movies within any given day of the week. This requires recognizing various constraints such as no two different movies starting at the same time (to minimize lobby congestion and smooth out concession labor), the minimum time between showings needed to make the screening room ready, and the opening/closing hours of the facility. Work by Eliashberg, Miller, Swami, Weinberg, and Wierenga (2003) has already begun in this direction.

The increased level of exhibition concentration and the appearance of new players also raise a number of important research issues such as development of differentiation strategies and managing a portfolio of entertainment assets and businesses. In a related vein, segmenting consumers based on their movie decision-making processes and analyzing the effectiveness of various consumer-relationship management strategies in the context of movie going are other areas, worth formal research.

## REFERENCES

Battaglio, Stephen, and Kirk Honeycutt. 1998. "Bronfman: Event Films Need Event Ticket Prices," *Hollywood Reporter*, April 1.

Brasell, R. Bruce. 1999. "Movie Exhibition Monopoly in Mobile No More: Diversity in Films Screened Promised," *The Harbinger* (Mobile, Alabama), February 23.

British Film Institute. "UK Box Office Breakdown 1995–2002." (Accessed from http:www.bfi.org.uk/facts/stats/index.html on 8/19/04.)

Caves, Richard E. 2000. *Creative Industries: Contracts between Art and Commerce,* Cambridge, MA: Harvard University Press.

Chisholm, Darlene C. 1997. "Profit-Sharing Versus Fixed-Payment Contracts: Evidence from the Motion Picture Industry," *Journal of Law, Economics & Organization,* 13(1): 169–201.

Credit Suisse First Boston. 2002. "Digital Cinema: Episode II," Sector Review: Americas/United States Imaging Technology, June 4. (Accessed from http://www.sabucat.com/digital.pdf on 3/28/04.)

Daniels, Bill, David Leedy, and Steven D. Sills. 1998. *Movie Money: Understanding Hollywood's (Creative) Accounting Practices,* Los Angeles, CA: Silman-James Press.

Davis, Peter. 2001. "Spatial Competition in Retail Markets: Movie Theaters," unpublished manuscript, Economics Department, London School of Economics, December.

———. 2003a. "The Effect of Local Competition on Retail Prices: The U.S. Motion Picture Exhibition Market," unpublished manuscript, Economics Department, London School of Economics, September.

————. 2003b. "Fine Young Cannibals in the U.S. Motion Picture Exhibition Market," unpublished manuscript, Economics Department, London School of Economics, October.

Diorio, Carl. 2003. "Regal Pumped for Hoyts' Haul," *Variety*, February 4.

Doyle, Barry. (1998). "Return of the Super Cinema (United Kingdom)," *History Today*, 48, February 1, pp. 2–4.

EAO (European Audiovisual Observatory). 2002. *Focus 2002: World Market Film Trends*. (Accessed from http://www.obs.coe.int/oea_publ/market/focus.html on 3/28/04.)

Einav, Liran, and Barak Y. Orbach. 2001. "Uniform Prices for Differentiated Goods: The Case of the Movie-Theater Industry," *Harvard Olin Discussion Paper* No. 337, October.

Elberse, Anita, and Jehoshua Eliashberg. 2003. "Demand and Supply for Sequentially Released Products in International Markets: The Case of Motion Pictures," *Marketing Science*, 22(3): 329–54.

Eliashberg, Jehoshua, Sanjeev Swami, Charles B. Weinberg, and Berend Wierenga. 2001. "Implementing and Evaluating SILVERSCREENER: A Marketing Management Support System for Movie Exhibitors," *Interfaces*, 31(3), Part 2 of 2, May–June, pp. S108–27.

Eliashberg, Jehoshua, Jedid-Jah Jonker, Mohanbir S. Sawhney, and Berend Wierenga. 2000. "MOVIEMOD: An Implementable Decision Support System for Pre-Release Market Evaluation of Motion Pictures," *Marketing Science*, 19(3): 226–43.

Eliashberg, Jehoshua, Steven J. Miller, Sanjeev Swami, Charles B. Weinberg, and Berend Wierenga. 2003. "Marketing Models for Movie Managers: Model Development and Implementation Experience," Marketing Science Conference, University of Maryland, June.

Eller, Claudia. 2002. "Showtime for Theater Owners: More Americans Went to Movies This Year than Anytime since 1959," *Los Angeles Times*, December 26.

Emmons, Natasha. 2001. "Game Works Enters Movie Theater Biz," *Amusement Business*, May 28.

Hanssen, Andrew F. 2002. "The Block-Booking of Films: A Re-Examination," *Journal of Law and Economic*, 43 (October): 395–426.

Hiltbrand, David. 2003. "TV Ads Play on the Big Screen," *Philadelphia Inquirer*, February 2.

Husted, Bryan W. 2000. "The Impact of National Culture on Software Piracy," *Journal of Business Ethics*, 26: 197–211.

Jones, J. Morgan, and Christopher J. Ritz. 1991. "Incorporating Distribution into New Product Diffusion Models," *International Journal of Research in Marketing*, 8 (June): 91–112.

Leenders, Mark A.A.M. and Jehoshua Eliashberg. 2004. "Antecedents and Consequences of Third-Party Products Evaluation Systems: Lessons from the International Motion Picture Industry," unpublished manuscript, Marketing Department, University of Pennsylvania Wharton School of Business.

Media Force. 2001. "Ten Top Pirated Movies in August [2001]," September 24. (Accessed from http://www.afterdawn.com/news/archive/2347.cfm on 3/28/04.)

Motion Picture Association of America website: http://www.mpaa.org

Sawhney, Mohanbir S., and Jehoshua Eliashberg. 1996. "A Parsimonious Model for Forecasting Gross Box-Office Revenues of Motion Pictures," *Marketing Science*, 15(2): 113–31.

*Screen Digest*. 2001. "Report on the Implications of Digital Technology for the Film Industry," UK, Department for Culture. Media and Sport, Creative Industries Division.

*Screen Digest Report*. 2002. "On the Implications of Digital Technology for the Film Industry," September. (Accessed from http://www.culture.gov.uk/PDF/Screen_Digest_Report.pdf on 3/28/04.)

Stigler, George. 1968. "A Note on Block-Booking," *The Organization of Industry*, Irwin Publishing Co.

Swami, Sanjeev, Jehoshua Eliashberg, and Charles B. Weinberg. 1999. "SILVERSCREENER: A Modeling Approach to Movie Screens Management," *Marketing Science*, 18(3): 352–72.

Swami, Sanjeev, Martin L. Puterman, and Charles B. Weinberg. 2001. "Play It Again, Sam? Optimal Replacement Policies for Motion Picture Retailing," *Manufacturing and Services Operations Management*, 3(4): 369–86.

Towira, Pimpaka. 2000. "Saturday Night at the Movies," *The Nation* (Thailand), July 18.

Valenti, Jack. 2001. "Valenti Warns of Potentially Devastating Economic Impact of Copyright Theft," MPAA press release, April 3. (Accessed from http://www.mpaa.org/jack/2001/2001_04_03a.htm on 3/28/04)

Vogel, Harold L. 2001. *Entertainment Industry Economics: A Guide for Financial Analysis*, Cambridge, UK, Cambridge University Press.

Wagner, Suzanne, C., and G. Lawrence Sanders. 2001. "Considerations in Ethical Decision-Making and Software Piracy," *Journal of Business Ethics*, 29: 161–67.

Weinstein, Mark. 1998. "Profit-Sharing Contracts in Hollywood: Evolution and Analysis," *Journal of Legal Studies*, January: 67–112.

# 6

# Profits out of the Picture: Research Issues and Revenue Sources Beyond the North American Box Office

**CHARLES B. WEINBERG**

Disney's *The Lion King* released in 1994 earned North American box revenues of $250 million, approximately a third of its total worldwide box office. Within 2 years, more than 50 million videos were sold, and retail merchandise sales exceeded $1.5 billion. *The Lion King* "isn't a movie. It's an industry."

(Hawkins, 1995)

Is a movie the primary product of Hollywood studios, or a "loss leader" for a stream of products that produces more than half the total revenue earned from each new Motion Picture Association of America (MPAA) release? According to data from the 2002 MPAA Economic Report (www.mpaa. org), the domestic box office totaled $9.5 billion, and the international box office gross was $9.6 billion, but the VHS and DVD rental and sales market totaled more than $20 billion.[1] Viewed alternatively, the average MPAA-released film in 2002 earned domestic box-office revenues of $32.5 million but cost $59 million to produce and another $31 million

---

[1] For historical reasons, "domestic" box-office revenue typically refers to revenues in both the United States and Canada.

The research assistance of Jason Ho and Shelley Ong in the preparation of this chapter is gratefully acknowledged.

Table 6.1: *2002 average revenues and costs.*

| Average box office | |
|---|---|
| MPAA new releases (220) | $32.5 Million |
| All new releases (449) | $21.2 Million |
| **Costs** | |
| MPAA new releases ($58.8 negative, $30.6 marketing) | $89.4 Million |
| MPAA subsidiary/affiliate ($34.0, $11.2) | $45.2 Million |

*Source:* 2002 MPAA Economic Report.

for distribution and marketing (Table 6.1). Although Hollywood studios acting as distributors earn profits from distribution, ancillary products are crucial by design for the success of Hollywood.[2]

This chapter has three objectives. The first is to establish the magnitude of the major ancillary products. The second is to examine the nature of the relationships among these markets. The third, and most important, is to raise a set of challenging research issues that is important from the standpoint of both academic researchers and industry professionals. Because the majority of ancillary revenue comes from the VHS and DVD rental and sales markets collectively referred to as the video market – the focus is on the video market.

In true movie fashion, here is a sneak preview. One of the most interesting issues, and an organizing framework for the research topics to be discussed, is the role of time in the movie industry. In brief, time is of the essence. Most mass-market movies follow a fairly standard time pattern. That is, as shown in Krider and Weinberg (1998), the first weekend of wide release achieves the highest attendance, and then attendance follows a fairly regular exponential decline after that (Figure 6.1). Although the actual opening and decay rates may vary, the pattern is very consistent. Moreover, Lehmann and Weinberg (2000) reported a similar result for

[2] Hollywood studios not only distribute their own movies, but also sometimes act as distributors of movies produced by others. For purposes of this chapter, I do not distinguish between these two cases and use the terms "distributors" and "Hollywood studios" interchangeably. That is consistent with usage in most industry studies.

Profits out of the Picture

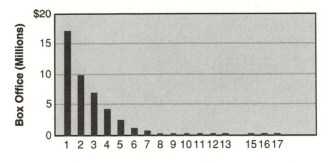

**Weeks Released**

*Don't Say a Word*, opening September 28, 2001, shows the
typical declining pattern of major movie releases.

Figure 6.1: Box-office pattern for a major movie. Weekly revenues of *Don't Say a Word*.

videos in a sample of thirty-five mid-'1990s movies (Figure 6.2). In addition, Lehmann and Weinberg found that a video's sales pattern was related to the movie's sales pattern.

The simplest question to ask is how long to wait after a movie is released to issue the video. If the video is released too long after the movie, then the excitement and hype surrounding the movie's release

**Combined Rentals of *Don't Say a Word***

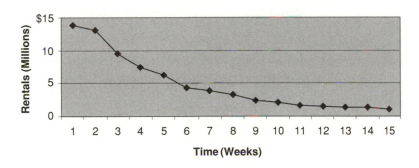

**Time (Weeks)**

\* Video/DVD release date of February 18, 2002.

Figure 6.2: Rental pattern for *Don't Say a Word*.

may well be dissipated. On the other hand, if the video is released very close to the movie's release date, then movie fans may feel that it is not worthwhile going to the movie and they should just see the video. In other words, to what extent does the movie serve as a promoter of the video, and to what extent does the video cannibalize box-office revenues? *Not only must the studio decide when to release the video, but it also must decide when to decide.* Should a movie studio decide the video release date prior to a movie's release date, or should it gather box-office data from the first few weeks and project video sales and then make a decision? Lehmann and Weinberg (2002) showed that there was considerable profit opportunity from varying video release times based on early box-office results.

Perhaps, however, the wrong question is being asked. At present, studios spend considerable effort determining the optimal opening date for their movies and then release the video about six months later (with limited variation). But, with the video market having twice the revenue of the box-office market, perhaps studios should optimize the video release date and then go backwards to determine the movie release date? Considering both release dates simultaneously would be a further step.

Moreover, if the video and movie are released close together, they are substitute products. If they are released farther apart, then they are complements – with many people who saw the movie choosing to view the video as well. So, when do these products change from being substitutes to complements?

### THE MANY MARKETS OF MOVIES

Disney's *The Lion King* (and also *Pocahontas*) is a classic example of a movie release designed to be successful not only in the North American box office, but also in a vast array of ancillary markets. Released June 14, 1994, for three months and then re-released for Thanksgiving, the revenue-generating products included consumer products (both Disney's own and licensed), theme-park attractions (within weeks of the movie's

Table 6.2: *Two Disney movies (values in $ million).*

|  | Pocahontas | The Lion King |
| --- | --- | --- |
| Production cost: | $60 Million | $60 Million |
| Domestic box office | 142 | 313 |
| International box office | 200 | 438 |
| TOTAL BOX OFFICE | 342 | 751 |
| Disney box-office share (50%) | 171 | 376 |
| Production & marketing cost | 40 | 90 |
| Box-office contribution | 131 | 286 |
| Domestic video contribution | 145 | 300 |
| International video | 85 | 200 |
| Consumer products | 198 | 225 |
| Direct-to-video contribution | 56 | 96 |
| TOTAL CONTRIBUTION | $555 | $1,047 |

*Source:* Reavis (1998).

release), video (first released in April 1995, for one year), television, books, direct-to-video sequels, and even a live theater show (1997). Of an estimated $1 billion in contribution to Disney, Table 6.2 shows that only about 15 percent came from the domestic box office. Although not as successful in dollar terms, *Pocahontas* had a similar result. (See Reavis 1998 for a detailed discussion of *The Lion King.*)

Children's movies, and particularly Disney children's movies, may be the pioneers in exploiting outside markets. However, the practice is now widespread. For example, consider Tables 6.3 and 6.4. For each of the past six years, the largest domestic box-office movie has had an even higher box office outside North America. The top ten domestic films of 2001 all had significant sales overseas.

Looking across the domestic industry in 2002, MPAA reports that video rentals totaled $8.2 billion in 2002 and video sales, $12.1 billion (Table 6.5). The most dramatic growth is in the DVD sales market, accounting for $8.7 billion and growing 53 percent over the previous year. With DVD player penetration at less than 40 percent of U.S. households at

Table 6.3: *U.S. vs. overseas box-office results.*

| | Movie revenues (millions) | |
|---|---|---|
| Movie title | Worldwide box office | Domestic box office |
| 2002: *Lord of the Rings: TTT* | $873 | $334 |
| 2001: *Harry Potter: Sorcerer's Stone* | $966 | $318 |
| 2000: *Mission Impossible II* | $545 | $215 |
| 1999: *Phantom Menace* | $922 | $431 |
| 1998: *Saving Private Ryan* | $480 | $216 |
| 1997: *Titanic* | $1835 | $600 |

Table 6.4: *Top 10 domestic box-office movies in 2001.*

| Movie title | Release date | Domestic box office | Foreign box office |
|---|---|---|---|
| *Harry Potter: Sorcerer's Stone* | 11/16/01 | $317.6 | $649.4 |
| *Lord of the Rings: Fellowship* | 12/19/01 | $313.3 | $547.2 |
| *Shrek* | 5/16/01 | $267.7 | $209.3 |
| *Monsters, Inc.* | 11/2/01 | $255.9 | $273.1 |
| *Rush Hour 2* | 8/3/01 | $226.2 | $102.7 |
| *The Mummy Returns* | 5/4/01 | $202.0 | $224.8 |
| *Pearl Harbor* | 5/25/01 | $198.5 | $251.5 |
| *Jurassic Park 3* | 7/8/01 | $181.2 | $184.7 |
| *Planet of the Apes* | 7/27/01 | $180.0 | $179.3 |
| *Hannibal* | 2/9/01 | $165.1 | $184.2 |

Table 6.5: *2002 domestic revenue results.*

| Venue | $Billion | (vs. 2001) |
|---|---|---|
| Domestic box office | $9.5 | (+13%) |
| DVD – Sales | $8.7 | (+53%) |
| DVD – Rentals | $2.9 | (+106%) |
| VHS – Sales | $3.4 | (−17%) |
| VHS – Rentals | $5.3 | (−25%) |

*Source:* 2002 MPAA Economic Report.

Table 6.6: *Media consumption – hours per person.*

| Filmed entertainment | 2002 | 2002/1998 |
|---|---|---|
| Cable + satellite TV | 851 | 1.28 |
| Broadcast TV | 810 | 0.92 |
| Internet | 157 | 2.90 |
| Home video | 77 | 2.14 |
| Box office | 13 | 1.00 |
| Other electronic entertainment | | |
| Radio | 1,001 | 1.07 |
| Recorded music | 228 | 0.81 |
| Video games | 84 | 1.95 |

*Source:* 2002 MPAA Economic Report.

the end of 2002 (but growing rapidly), this market can only become more significant.

According to MPAA data, the average consumption per person of box-office entertainment is 13 hours per year, compared to 77 hours per year of home video. Both these numbers are dwarfed by the 1,661 hours per year spent watching TV (Table 6.6). In 2002, foreign box office in total was approximately equal to the U.S. box office (Groves 2003).[3] Although the 2002 result is due in part to currency fluctuations, the foreign market is a significant addition to the domestic box office. Although data on the price that television stations pay for individual feature films is difficult to obtain in general, industry trade publications estimate that the networks pay approximately 15 percent of domestic box office for the rights for the first three to four showings of feature films (March 10, 2003).[4] Pay per view and video on demand, although

[3]  Of course, Hollywood studios receive only part of these gross revenues. Hollywood's share, termed "rentals," totaled $3.6 billion for the domestic market and $3.1 billion for the international market in 2002 (Groves 2003). Distribution fees and other charges are additional sources of income. Industry sources frequently estimate Hollywood's share as about 50% of box-office revenue.

[4]  Global sales of feature films, made-for-TV movies, television series, and other products were $11 billion ($7.2 billion in the United States) to free television. Global

possibly the wave of the future, are still important but smaller sources of revenue. The value of product licensing agreements also adds to the total revenues that flow from a movie. Particular films may also have special markets that can be developed. Movies such as *Spiderman* have impressive tie-ins with the comic-book industry; other movies are the source (or even the result) of interactive video games.[5] Although all these markets are important, as indicated previously, this chapter concentrates on the video market, as that – along with foreign box office – is the most significant revenue stream beyond the domestic box office.

## RELATIONSHIPS MATTER

### Overseas Box-Office Results

Not surprisingly, foreign box-office results are correlated with the North American box office. For a sample of 175 major movies released between 1991 and 1993, Ravid and Basuroy (2004) found a correlation of $r = 0.86$ for total box office in the two markets, as seen in Table 6.7.[6] Although until fairly recently, Hollywood studios typically released their movies overseas many months after their North American release, often utilizing returned prints from North American theaters, the cause-and-effect relationship between these two markets can be questioned. Do, for example, North American and overseas audiences have similar tastes, so that whatever movies do well in North American do well overseas? Whereas there is some argument as to whether or not all genres traveled equally well (comedy may be less cross-cultural than action movies),

---

sales to pay television were $3.3 billion ($1.5 billion in the United States) (Groves 2003).

[5] For example, coincident with the release of *Spiderman*, the comic-book industry launched massive promotions in which participating retailers gave away a free comic book to everyone coming to their stores.

[6] Suman Basuroy's assistance in providing correlation statistics is gratefully acknowledged. Other variables, such as MPAA rating (e.g., PG, R), can further help in estimating this relationship. Jedidi et al. (1998) present a data-based approach to grouping movies.

Table 6.7: *Domestic box office and foreign box office.*

| Source | Result |
| --- | --- |
| 1991–1993 $n = 175$. Ravid & Basuroy (2003) | $r = 0.86$ for total box office |
| 1999 $n = 156$ films released in U.S. and Europe. Elberse & Eliashberg (2003) | Foreign opening week box office significantly related to (+) U.S. performance (−) Time Lag * U.S. performance |
| 2001 top 100 movies (domestic box office) $n = 86$ | $r = 0.88$ for total box office |

the possible universality of movie audience tastes can be hypothesized as an explanation for the observed correlations. In addition, the large production budgets of Hollywood films may so dominate the spending level of locally produced films that they dominate local markets in the same proportion as they did in North America.[7] Another argument is that the advertising and word-of-mouth campaigns developed around North American movies directly or indirectly influenced attendance in other markets as well.

More recently, many Hollywood movies have been released almost simultaneously in North America and in at least some major markets. Reasons for these new timing strategies include a more global management view, fear of piracy, and the desire to utilize worldwide satellite television and Internet media to take advantage of the intensive launch marketing campaigns. In a study of 156 Hollywood movies released in North America in 1999 and also in four European countries, Elberse and Eliashberg (2003) found that U.S. performance (defined as the average

---

[7] Waterman and Lee (2002a) indicate that the average 1995 U.S. movie in their sample cost $12.3 million to produce, whereas the average movies made in the United Kingdom, France, Japan, Germany, and Italy cost, respectively, $6.0, $4.7, $4.3, $4.1, and $2.7 million to produce.

per screen revenues in the first two weeks) was significantly related to overseas opening-week box office. Moreover, this relationship was mediated by the delay between the U.S. and the foreign opening: The longer the delay, the weaker the impact of U.S. performance (the U.S. performance also affected number of screens). This suggests that something more than similarity of audiences is at play.

More directly, the present paper analyzes total North American and foreign box office for the hundred largest box-office films in the United States in 2001.[8] As expected, a significant $r = 0.88$ was obtained. Further analysis to investigate the effect of genre and release time on the relationship between domestic and foreign box offices would be interesting. Management attention to worldwide and not just U.S. box office is well justified both by the magnitude of the markets and the relationship between them.

## Video Markets

Not surprisingly, Ravid and Basuroy's data for the early 1990s also showed a strong relationship of $r = 0.70$ for domestic box-office and video revenues (Table 6.8). Analyzing data for thirty-five movies and videos from 1994 and 1995, Lehmann and Weinberg found that a video's opening strength and decay rate were significantly related to a movie's box-office performance. At that time, the majority of the video business for major movies was concentrated on the rental, not purchase, of videos. For example, 70 percent of the movies in Lehmann and Weinberg's sample had a retail price of $70 or more. With the exception of children's movies and some selected titles, the underlying assumption was that consumers were primarily interested in renting videos for one-time viewing at home. (A research question that requires further examination is whether the renters

---

[8] Data on foreign box office, video tape rentals, and DVD rentals are available for 86 of the top 100 domestic box-office films of 2001. This sample is used throughout this chapter unless otherwise noted.

Table 6.8: *Domestic box office and video market.*

| Source | Result |
|---|---|
| 1991–1993 $n = 175$<br>Ravid & Basuroy (2003) | $r = 0.70$ for box-office and total video revenues |
| 1994–1995 $n = 35$<br>Lehmann & Weinberg (2000) | Weekly revenues $= A * \exp(-Bt)$<br>Video opening significantly related to<br>$(+)$ movie opening<br>$(-) *$ movie decay<br>Video decay rate significantly related to<br>$(+)$ movie opening |
| 2001 $n = 86$ of top 100 movies | Domestic box office and<br>$r = 0.40$ video tape rental<br>$r = 0.24$ DVD rental |
| 2002<br>$n = 35$ of top 50 video sellers<br>$n = 42$ of top 50 video sellers | Domestic box office and<br>$r = 0.55$ video tape sales<br>$r = 0.81$ DVD sales |

wanted to repeat an experience they had in a movie theater or to see a movie that they had "missed" during its [usually short] box-office run.)

DVDs – and the movie studios' interest in purchase (termed "sell-through") rather than rental – changed all that. In 1997, the MPAA estimates there were only six-hundred movie titles available in DVD; by 2002, that number exceeded twenty-thousand. With an average price of $20.78 in 2002, the consumer "sell-through" market is now a major focus for movie producers. Although a video tape is primarily the movie in another delivery system, the DVD has a set of enhancements that potentially make it a different product in consumers' minds. The growth in sales of DVDs (as compared to VHS cassettes) is consistent with the distinctive view. Moreover, the results for rentals and sales appear to differ. For example, there is virtually no overlap between the top ten rentals of 2002 and the top ten selling videos of 2002 in either the VHS or DVD market. Moreover, as discussed more fully in the next paragraph, the relationship between the rental market and the box-office market is no longer as

Table 6.9: *Top rental titles of 2002.*

| Movie title | Combined revenue $ Million | DVD revenue $ Million | VHS revenue $ Million | Release date | Domestic box-office |
|---|---|---|---|---|---|
| *Don't Say a Word* | $83.97 | $28.54 | $55.44 | 02/19/02 | $55.0 |
| *Ocean's Eleven* | $82.20 | $33.39 | $48.81 | 05/07/02 | $183.4 |
| *Training Day* | $79.52 | $30.32 | $49.20 | 03/19/02 | $76.3 |
| *The Fast & the Furious* | $70.71 | $22.22 | $48.49 | 01/02/02 | $144.5 |
| *The Others* | $64.46 | $25.35 | $39.11 | 05/14/02 | $96.5 |

strong as it formerly was. For the top 2001 movies Lehmann and Weinberg studied, they obtained a correlations of $r = 0.40$ between domestic box office and VHS rentals and $r = 0.24$ between domestic box office and DVD rentals. Data are available from videobusiness.com for the fifty best-selling VHS tapes and the fifty best-selling DVDs. Consequently, to analyze video sales, Lehmann and Weinberg started not with the leading box-office figures but with the fifty top VHS tapes and DVDs of 2002. Only thirty-five of these VHS tape best sellers are also on the domestic box office list of one-hundred leading movies; forty-two of the DVDs are (many of the missing titles were direct-to-video releases). Using this as a base, Lehmann and Weinberg find correlations of $r = 0.55$ and $r = 0.81$ between domestic box office and VHS and DVD sales, respectively.

As the leading rental video of 2002 would indicate, the relationship between the box-office and home-viewing markets is far from automatic or given (See Tables 6.9 and 6.10). The top-renting 2002 video, *Don't Say a Word*, a thriller movie starring Michael Douglas, earned only $55 million in box-office revenues and received mixed reviews when it was released. While speculation about the reason for this particular video's success is beyond the scope of this chapter, there appear to be systematic differences in box-office and video performance, and management actions make a difference. As noted earlier, Lehmann and Weinberg show that the time

Table 6.10: *Top selling titles of 2002.*

| Movie title | Combined revenue | DVD revenue $ Million | VHS revenue $ Million | Release date | Domestic box office |
|---|---|---|---|---|---|
| *Monsters, Inc.* | $347 | $202.0 | $145.2 | 09/17/02 | $255.9 |
| *Lord of the Rings: Fellowship* | $330 | $257.3 | $72.8 | 08/06/02 | $313.3 |
| *Spiderman* | $299 | $215.3 | $84.0 | 11/01/02 | $403.7 |
| *Harry Potter & the Sorcerer's Stone* | $298 | $166.7 | $81.7 | 12/03/02 | $145.8 |
| *Ice Age* | $203 | $124.8 | $78.1 | 11/26/02 | $176.4 |

between video and movie release affects the rentals of a movie. Moreover, the use of sell-through pricing influences the stocking policy of retailers, which indirectly influences video rentals. According to Lehmann and Weinberg, sell-through videos tend to open more strongly and decay more rapidly.

Mortimer (2004) conducted a more systematic test of the effect of contract terms on video retailer performance. Prior to 1998, home-video retailers paid distributors approximately $70 per video tape and retained all receipts. Starting in 1998, many distributors offered a new contract in which the retailer paid an upfront fee of $3 to $8 per movie and retained about 45 percent of revenues. This change allowed retailers to stock many more copies of new videos, with a consequent increase in consumer satisfaction and a change in advertising strategy of emphasizing movie availability. According to Mortimer's analysis, total distributor and retailer profits increased by 3 to 6 percent, and consumers were better off.

Management action, as indicated previously and unsurprisingly, influences a video's performance. Management action also leads to the deviation between box-office performance and video performance. Management designs DVDs with enhanced features that may appeal both to a gift-buying market and to people who may want to collect a large or a small set of DVDs. Such markets may have different evaluative criteria than the box-office market, so that titles that perform well in one market may not perform well in another.

Consumer behavior may explain why some of the most successful video rentals are not box-office successes. With movie admissions averaging $5.81 per ticket (MPAA) in 2002 and video rentals at about $3 ($3.20 for DVD, $2.70 for VHS) (www.vsda.org, January 9, 2003), people may assign movies to theater and home-video categories. Viewers eager to see Oscar-nominated and award-winning movies may be too late to see them in theaters. Additionally, people may wish to view certain movies in the privacy of their homes.[9]

### ANALYZE THIS: RESEARCH ISSUES

The movie industry in general and the auxiliary market in particular provide a number of interesting research challenges. In this chapter, I highlight two main issues and then discuss some other topics. The first issue – the timing game – examines the relationship between the movie and the video markets, especially the issue of how long the distributor should wait between releasing the movie and the video (the video window). In this section, the primary research approach involves analytical marketing models. The second issue – the purchase experience – considers what happens in the video rental store. Videos are an unusual product in that most consumers enter a video store definitely knowing that they will be renting a video but not knowing which video they will rent. In addition, most renters are renting for multiple viewers but not all are in the store simultaneously. Consequently, there are problems of multiple buyers and agency. Although both of these research examples concentrate on the video rental market, the growing importance of video sales

---

[9]  Adult videos, which are primarily released as direct-to-video or pay-per-view markets, rarely obtain widespread release in theaters and, consequently, are not studied in this chapter.

MANUFACTURER        CHANNEL        ULTIMATE CUSTOMER

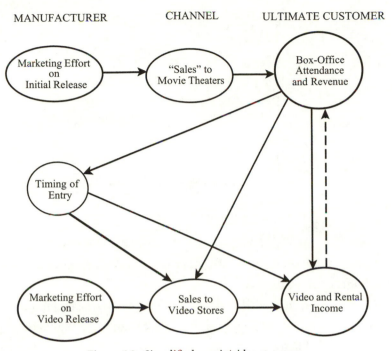

Figure 6.3: Simplified movie/video structure.

(particularly DVDs) will raise new and interesting questions for both researchers and managers.

## The Timing Game

The size of the window between a movie's theatrical release and its release on video is one of the studio's most critical decisions for the ancillary markets (See Figure 6.3). Releasing a movie on video shortly after theatrical release ensures that consumer interest generated by memory of the original advertising campaign and potentially positive word of mouth will still be strong. A quick video release, however, also risks cannibalizing theatrical sales through a lower margin outlet. The following discussion (taken from Lehmann and Weinberg [2002] and formally supplemented

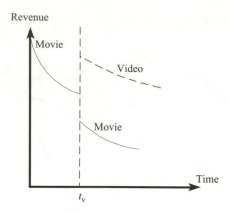

Figure 6.4: Movie and video demand patterns.

by an Appendix) shows how different factors affect the proper balance in the timing of video release.

There is now substantial evidence supporting the idea that movie demand both in theaters and video stores can be closely approximated with an exponential function on the age of the movie: $Q = Ae^{-m^*Age}$. The parameter $A$ captures a movie's popularity, whereas $m$ captures the speed of decay. Such a function implies that demand falls by a constant percentage with each passing week (See Figure 6.4). Video demand largely follows the prior exponential demand specification. It differs in that a video's popularity is influenced by box-office attendance and by the size of the window between theatrical and video release (the bigger the window, the lower the demand), and the relevant age is time since video release. Video demand falls with the length of release delay largely because potential customers have either "purchased" it (i.e., saw the movie in theaters) or forgotten the communication effort surrounding the movie's introduction. Although the following general story holds for any demand that decreases over time, the precise conclusions are based on this exponential specification.

Empirically gauging the cannibalization of theatrical sales by video sales is difficult because one never observes the simultaneous (or even nearby) release of a movie in theaters and on video. Given the standard window of five to six months, though, it appears that video release completely forecloses theatrical sales. For the movies studied in Lehmann and Weinberg, theatrical revenues at video release never exceeded 3 percent of first-week's revenue.

If the studio directly controlled the video retailer, a framework that incorporated both theatrical and video profits would capture the most critical aspect of the decision problem. Video retailers, however, are independent of distributors. Lehmann and Weinberg model the dominant case of the mid-1990s in which the movie distributor earns income from the videos purchased by the retailer rather than as a share of the rental revenue.[10] The number of units the retailer orders should depend on the estimated demand for video rentals. Importantly, video demand is assumed to be predictable based on demand in the first channel (i.e., box-office attendance) and to depend on entry timing. Given these assumptions, distributors will consider the optimal retailer reactions when setting their video-release window. In addition, distributors can make more accurate forecasts if they wait to make the video-window decisions until they observe several weeks of box-office sales.

This model, of course, captures just some aspects of the decision problem. In addition to relations with video stores, movie producers' concerns include tie-in promotional merchandise, relations with independently owned theaters, and timing vis-à-vis other releases. Furthermore, the model does not capture the likely gradual but potentially important adaptation by consumers to release strategies through expectation-setting and its consequences.

### Retailers' Optimal Order Quantity

An independent video retailer faces its own balancing act. A profit-maximizing video store must trade off the foregone marginal profit from

---

[10] Although rental sharing began to occur around 1997 (see Mortimer 2004), the model and concepts can readily be modified to account for this shift in industry practice.

being understocked with the purchase and holding costs of an additional copy. Although a retailer may in theory reorder at any time, the declining demand for movies makes it almost always optimal to order a video exclusively at release. Also note that a retailer facing decreasing demand is unlikely to order enough videos to satisfy demand in the initial periods.

When the retailer is understocked, the number of times a particular title is rented is the product of the number of tapes and the turnover rate (e.g., three per week), whereas when overstocked, the number is simply the original demand for the video. The time after the video's release when demand equals the rental capacity can be found by setting the two numbers equal. Assuming that unsatisfied demand due to capacity constraints leads to lost sales and/or dissatisfied customers, the optimal quantity of videos for a retailer to buy behaves intuitively. Retailers' quantity ordered decreases with the price per copy and increases with the rental fee that retailers charge. Whereas the relationship between the quantity ordered and the turnover rate is theoretically ambiguous, parameter estimates indicate an inverse relationship between quantity and the turnover rate. Finally, and most importantly, the retailer quantity is decreasing in the size of the video-release window.

## Manufacturer's (Distributor's) Optimal Release Time to the Retailer

With the video stores' response to time of release in terms of quantity in hand, I now turn to the issue of the movie distributor's optimal decision with respect to release time (See Figure 6.5). Lehmann and Weinberg assume distributor profits in the movie channel are proportional to the number of attenders and, in the video channel, proportional to the number of videos bought by retailers.

The distributor's cumulative profit function can then be expressed as the simple sum of the profit from the theatrical market and the profit from the video market. Delaying the video release increases theatrical profits and decreases video profits. From the optimal solution to the

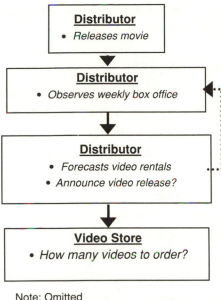

Note: Omitted
- *Other sequential channels*
- *Sales of video*

Figure 6.5: Decision structure.

distributor's problem, Lehmann and Weinberg confirm a great deal of intuition and gain some insight. The bigger and more profitable the movie market is relative to the video market, the greater the optimal delay in the video's release. The more rapid the video's implicit decay before its release, the earlier the optimal video release. Further, the more the decay of the theatrical movie exceeds the implicit decay of the video, the earlier the video should be released.

The effect of price (to the retailer) on the optimal release time is complex. On the one hand, increasing the price makes the video more profitable per video sold, decreasing the time to release the video. On the other hand, the video stores order fewer videos facing the higher price, increasing the optimal release-window size. This effect contrasts starkly with the rental fee. The video store's ability to increase its rental fee unambiguously leads to higher video profits, higher orders, and an earlier release date.

## Data and Variables

Lehmann and Weinberg compiled data for a convenience sample of thirty-five movies released from January 1994 through August 1995. They obtained strong empirical support for the exponential models discussed previously, with average $R^2$s of 0.90 and 0.86, respectively, for theatrical movies and videos.

The impact of decision variables can be captured by allowing the parameters that describe the popularity and the decay of theatrical movie demand to depend on distributor choices. Because the vast majority of marketing expenditures occur before a movie is released, Lehmann and Weinberg reduce the set of distributor choices to a one-time pre-launch advertising expenditure. Video demand should also potentially depend on marketing expenditures and box-office performance, as such "carryover" might be an important factor in distributor decision making.

This carryover is captured by allowing the parameters that describe the hypothetical "simultaneous release" popularity of the video and the post-release decay to depend on other variables. Here, these variables include the theatrical-demand parameters, the delay between theatrical and video release, and other decision variables.

Once the movie's run commences, a number of strategies can be employed to extend the movie's run. Lehmann and Weinberg examine two marketing decisions concerning the release of a film on video. The first is the time between the movie's release and the video's release. As discussed previously, a longer delay until the video's release reduces the likelihood that the movie's sales will be cannibalized by the video. Pressure for delay is mirrored by the common practice in the book industry of delaying the paperback's release until the hardcover version has relatively small sales. On the other hand, when sequential product entry is delayed substantially from the release of the original product, advertising and publicity effects that surrounded the release of the movie will have largely dissipated.

Despite the potentially strong effects of a delay in a video's release on video rentals, Lehmann and Weinberg find relatively limited variation in the length of time between the movie's release and the video's release. The average for the thirty-five movies in the study was 23.8 weeks with a standard deviation of 3.5 weeks, resulting in a coefficient of variation much lower than that for any of the other variables studied.[11] Moreover, the lag is minimally correlated with either the movie's theatrical popularity ($r = 0.07$, $p > 0.10$) or its rate of decay ($r = -0.16$, $p > 0.10$), which suggests that movie studios do not change their release strategy for videos even after they have knowledge of the sales pattern of their movies. Most important, perhaps due to the attenuation in range, release time is significantly related to neither the video's potential popularity ($r = -0.05$, $p > 0.10$) nor its rate of decay ($r = -0.07$, $p > 0.10$).

A second variable of interest when a video is released is pricing. At the time of Lehmann and Weinberg's study, two price points appear to have been used in practice. One, a wholesale price of $60 or more to video stores, is designed with the expectation that the primary market for the video will be rentals. The second, however, a wholesale price of $20 or less, is designed to encourage the *sell-through* market.

In Lehmann and Weinberg's data, the opening strength of a movie is significantly related ($r = 0.42$, $p < 0.05$) to the use of a sell-through video price; theatrical decay rate is not ($r = -0.04$, $p > 0.10$). Movies that

---

[11] In a more extensive analysis of 1,429 movies released between 1988 and 1997, Waterman and Lee (2002b) report a mean (and median) "window" of 180 days with a slight down trend over time. While there is variation in the length of the window, 68.5% of videos are released within ±18 days (10%) of the median window. The variance of length of window is 1,930 days compared with a mean window of 184 days. The standard deviation for the total box office is $34.7 million compared to a mean of $27.2 million. For the top 100 movies studied in this chapter, the mean video window was 168 days (24 weeks) with a standard deviation of 37. There is far more variation in box-office strength than there is in length of the video window.

have high opening box offices are more likely to employ a sell-through strategy. Not surprisingly, the use of a sell-through strategy is significantly correlated with the video's potential strength ($r = 0.64$, $p < 0.01$) and its video decay rate ($r = 0.67$, $p < 0.01$).

### *Optimal Release Policy for Individual Movies*

Lehmann and Weinberg examine the determinants of the video's opening strength (denoted by $v_1$) and the video's decay rate (denoted by $v_2$). Theatrical opening strength ($m_1{}^B$) and the decay of theatrical demand ($m_2$) are taken from earlier estimation. Lehmann and Weinberg obtain the following regression equations (omitting error terms and other variables) to estimate the video's opening strength and decay rate:

$$v_1 = 24.46 + 0.556m_1^B + 19.86m_2$$
$$v_2 = 0.04 + .000557m_1^B + 0.01m_2$$

In addition to sell-through pricing, as discussed previously, all the reported variables are significant at the level $p = 0.05$ except for the effect of the movie decay rate on the video decay rate.

Based on a series of assumptions to estimate market size and profitability parameters, Lehmann and Weinberg derive optimal release times for the twenty-five videos that were released for the non–sell-through market. To illustrate, *Cool-Runnings* had a relatively weak opening (as compared to other movies) but a slow decay in the theater. On the other hand, its performance in the video market was typical of that for the non–sell-through movies in the sample. Lehmann and Weinberg estimate that the optimal time to release *Cool Runnings* would be ten weeks after its movie release, eleven weeks earlier than its actual release time of twenty-one weeks. This could have potentially increased the studio's profit by an estimated 8 percent. Overall, the general recommendation of Lehmann and Weinberg's analysis is to release videos earlier and also to allow for variation in video release times of between three and ten weeks.

The particular parameter values for each movie determine the appropriate release date. Institutional restrictions, legal constraints, competitive considerations, and consumer expectations may limit the feasibility and reasonableness of decreasing the time to video release as fully as suggested in the analysis, but the directional implications are quite strong.

## Research Questions and Issues

As argued earlier, in the movie/video business, time is of the essence. The previously analysis not only indicates the importance of time itself, but also the time of decision-making. Although many research issues and questions follow from this analysis, I focus on what Hollywood might call the *Magnificent Seven*.

*1. Simultaneous versus sequential (which comes first) decision making.* The previous models assume that the time of theatrical release is fixed and that the video-release timing decision can be made sequentially. An alternative approach, especially important given that the video market is twice as large as the domestic box office, is to decide first on the time of the video release and then work forward to determine the time of the movie's release. Krider and Weinberg (1998) extensively analyse the competitive movie timing game for movie releases, and the trade press frequently reports on this, but perhaps the more critical timing game concerns video release. Such a view would require different types of parameter estimation approaches than those used by Lehmann and Weinberg. An even more comprehensive extension would simultaneously consider the optimal timing of release in the theater and the video channels. One complexity to include would be the potential value of information from sales in one channel for determining sales in other channels. The role of marketing variables in influencing sales patterns directly or indirectly would be particularly interesting. Elberse and Eliashberg (2003), for example, study the effect of distribution intensity (number of screens) on the box-office results in domestic and foreign markets.

*2. Great (Customer) Expectations.* If the timing of release of products to sequential markets changes radically, then the issue of customer expectations needs to be considered. If a potential moviegoer knows a movie is likely to be released only five weeks after its theater release, then the likelihood of going to a theater to see the movie may be decreased.

From another perspective, Prasad, Bronnenberg, and Mahajan's (2004) game theoretic analysis suggests that one reason for the relatively uniform release time for videos is to avoid strategic behavior where competing firms, anticipating consumer response, move up release times so that movie and video release times eventually become simultaneous. Waterman and Lee (2002b) note that the relatively long window between a movie's release and a video's release suggests "the plausibility of some form of coordinated video window setting behavior among U.S. distributors as a means of coping with the time consistency problem" (p. 5).

Interestingly, industry practice in the movie industry appears to be changing. In the summer of 2001, in contrast to historical practice and likely motivated by the recent expansion of theater capacity, movies were released with a much larger number of initial screens (sometimes totalling more than 3,500) – resulting in relatively high opening weekends but fast decay rates and less time in theaters. If such policies persist, different sequential distribution strategies will be needed. As indicated earlier, the average time between movie release and video release is declining.

*3. Role of intermediate products.* As the examples of the two Disney movies at the start of the chapter indicate, movies often lend themselves to the generation of a wide range of products. A narrow view would be that each product is a profit generator in its own right, obviously drawing on the appeal of the originating element – typically the movie but ranging from video games to song titles to books. However, a product-line view might be more appropriate with an attempt to understand to what extent one product form is a substitute for the other and to what extent it is a complement. Moreover, certain products may serve indirectly as part of the marketing communication mix for a movie, its sequel, or the video. Thus, a video game released between the movie and video may serve as a reminder and preserve awareness of the movie title. Just as managers in the music industry need to decide whether or not to release a single to promote an album's sales, movie management needs to determine what and how many intermediate products to release and when to release them. Models from the advertising literature concerning continuous versus pulsed advertising strategies may be relevant here.

4. *Risky Business – Model uncertainty directly.* The movie industry, if nothing else, is a *Risky Business.* More generally, incorporating uncertainty explicitly in the demand functions and allowing for heterogeneity across retailers (e.g., a "ma and pa" versus mega-store segmentation) may also prove interesting. In the area of scheduling movies into theaters, Swami, Puterman, and Weinberg (2001) show the effect of uncertainty on optimal scheduling policies using a Markov Decision Process approach.

5. *Forecasting issues.* One key implication of the high correlations between the theater and video parameters is that good estimates of the video's two parameters are possible early in the sales curve for theaters. These estimates would likely be even more accurate if a meta-analysis of parameters for other movies were incorporated into the forecasting routine. Examining the issue dynamically, parameter estimates could be updated with weekly or daily box-office results. Hence, an interesting research (and managerial) question concerns deciding whether to postpone releasing a video until more information about theater revenues becomes available. That is, in order to decide whether to introduce the product to the second channel after each period of data, one needs to compute the expected profits of staying in theaters and moving to videos. The profits in turn, are a direct function of the parameters. Further departing from a strict forecasting view, marketing decisions can influence the parameter values.

Incorporation of primary market research data into the estimation would be useful, as Eliashberg et al. (2000) have demonstrated. However, a challenge in this area, as discussed in the next section, is that consumers frequently select and view videos in groups, so that an understanding of how to combine individual preferences to obtain a joint preference is required. One speculation is that people renting in groups are more likely to select less popular box-office movies in order to minimize the likelihood of a group member having seen the movie.

6. *Number of channel members.* Lehmann and Weinberg analyze only two sequential channels and assume the sequence is known and that the channels are independent. The issue of degree of vertical integration is controversial and worthy of investigation. Although some issues could be answered in Lehmann and Weinberg's framework (e.g., what if the distributors also owned the video retailers?), others require a different approach. Whereas adding more channels to the model is relatively straightforward, the problem of determining the appropriate sequence of channels is more complex, especially with regard to different patterns of cannibalization across channels. In addition, structural constraints such as contractual obligations and channel relationships need investigation.

7. *Channel management issues.* Mortimer (2004) has shown how the changing contract terms between the distributors and retailers have had a substantial impact on revenues and profits. With the growing importance of video sales through new channels, substantial opportunities for research are available. These areas are particularly intriguing because, quite often, the objective function for the channel members may not be profit maximization for the movies. For example, mass merchandisers may offer deep discounts on DVDs to drive store traffic. With many major studios now owned by global conglomerates, perhaps it could be argued that few businesses in the supply chain actually derive their main profits from the movie itself.

## The Video Store Experience

There are many ways in which a person or group of persons can acquire access to a film. These include the following:

- going to a movie theater
- renting a video at a video store
- purchasing a video at a video store
- purchasing a video at a nonspecialist retailer
- watching it on television (pay-per-view, premium cable, or broadcast)

The focus here is on renting a video, although all the areas have particular points of interest. In some ways, going to a theater and renting a video are similar experiences as they both involve primarily the short-term experience of seeing a movie and are usually done not individually but in groups of two or more – requiring a balancing of individual preferences. However, they also differ in important ways. As discussed herein, whereas people generally go to a movie theater knowing the specific movie that they intend to see, the majority of renters do not know what specific movie they will rent as they enter the video store. Moreover, typically the people who actually go to the video store are acting as "agents" for the people who will be viewing the video tape.

To provide some preliminary data on the video store, a market research survey was conducted on Saturday night, February 15, 2003, the first Saturday on which the widely anticipated *My Big Fat Greek Wedding* was available on video. The survey was conducted as people entered and left a local affiliate of a major national chain of video stores in a residential neighborhood in Vancouver, Canada. There were forty-nine completed surveys, with 52 percent male and an average age of thirty-three years.

Although 28 percent of the store's customers visited the video store alone, only 12 percent intended to watch alone (Table 6.11). Alternatively viewed, 35 percent of renters were making choices for people who were not in the store with them. This problem of agency would not

Table 6.11: *The video store experience.*

Survey: Saturday, February 15, 2003
Entry/Exit ($n = 50$)
Percentage of People

|  | Renting | Viewing |
|---|---|---|
| Alone | 28% | 12% |
| With 1 person | 38% | 36% |
| With 2 persons | 18% | 24% |
| With 3 persons | 14% | 28% |
| | | |
| Intentions entering the store | | |
| Rent *My Big Fat Greek Wedding* | 25% | |
| Rent another specific title | 25% | |
| Rent, but no specific title | 50% | |

be a serious one if renters had beforehand decided on what video to rent. Even on a night when *My Big Fat Greek Wedding* debuted (25 percent of customers who entered the store intended to rent it), 50 percent of renters did not have a specific title in mind when they entered the store. Most renters intended to rent only one video and, on the exit poll, they did so. Everyone who intended to rent a video as they entered the store did so, although of the 40 percent intending to rent a DVD, only 34 percent actually left with a DVD. About 30 percent of respondents rented more videos than they originally intended. Satisfaction with the retail experience was 4.3 out of 5, based on responses at the exit interview.

Although at the aggregate level, overall video rental demand can be fairly well predicted near the time of video release, the individual or group behavior decision is not well understood. Moreover, even with the revenue-sharing agreements now in place between video distributors and video retailers, the newest videos are unlikely to be held in sufficient supply to meet demand. To provide contrast with the first research section on the Timing Game, this section focuses on questions at the individual level. These *Five* (not so) *Easy Pieces* are as follows:

*1. When are preferences formed?* At some stage, potential viewers have made a definite commitment to rent a video. No one in our sample went to the video store just to browse. However, the specificity of that commitment may be gradually narrowed over time, or it may be postponed until the video store is entered. Clearly, given that most people entering the store do not have a specific movie in mind, the environment of the video store will have a strong influence on preferences and choice.

*2. What is the role of recognition, recall, attitude, and preference, and how do they decay over time?* A video store is nothing if not a vast display of movie billboards in miniature. Because recognition, or the processes underlying it, decays more slowly than that of recall, for example, understanding the role of each of these constructs in the video choice decision is important.

*3. How are individual preferences or utilities established?* There are well-established models of utility for hedonic products. Probably, the novel aspects of this environment are the issues of how individual utilities are adjusted, if at all, for the presumed utilities of others and the updating of utilities as new information is obtained in the video store itself.

The video store would be an interesting test laboratory for the study of the effects of word of mouth and of peer pressure on consumer behavior. Combining in-store experiments with entry and exit polls, as was reported previously, provides a fruitful real world laboratory for the study of effects important both to the movie market in particular and consumer research more generally.

Another aspect concerns whether people who had seen the movie previously are more or less likely to want to see the video. This relationship, of course, would be mediated by the movie itself; fans of *The Matrix*, for example, eagerly awaited the DVD's release. In certain "franchise films," fans may want to experience the film's effects in a variety of different product forms. Disney's *The Lion King*, as discussed earlier, exemplifies this phenomena and a product line designed to meet this need.

*4. How are joint decisions made?* Whether in the theater or at home, few people (attend or) rent a movie to view it alone. As compared to the vast body of research on individual decision making, relatively little is known about how joint-decisions are made. One argument, at least in this environment, would be an adaptation of an elimination rule. At the extreme, if anyone in the group has seen the movie, then the video is not rented. This would tend to support, as discussed earlier, the notion of "second-chance" movies – some "Film flops flourish on DVD, VHS" (www.cnn.com, March 11, 2003). Also, newer videos are less likely to be seen by group members.

At the level of the joint decision, if previous viewing does not eliminate a movie, does the individual who has seen the movie carry more weight in the joint-decision process? Is this, in a sense, the ultimate in word of mouth? What weight do others place on the individual's opinion, the need not to see a video again (discussed previously), and the availability of other alternatives?

One moderating influence is the composition of the group. Couples and close friends who regularly view movies together may have a more long-term perspective and know the preferences of other group members better than do groups comprising people who only seldom view movies together.

In summary, if one knew the individual utility functions of the group members, what additional processes would need to be understood in order to know the group's joint-utility function? And, how would this relate to choice?

*5. What is the effect of agency?* As the previous data illustrate, only some of the people who are going to view the video go to the store to rent the video. Because typically only one video is rented and the product is consumed almost immediately, the renters act as agents for the viewers. Whereas the dollar and time commitments involved in this behavior are relatively low, the impact of such agency behavior would be interesting to study. The agents may be operating under constraints (e.g., rent anything but a horror film) either explicit or implicit. Are the agency effects similar to those involved in going from an individual to a joint decision, or does the agency issue add further complexity to the choice process?

## Other Research Issues

There are many other research issues raised with regard to the auxiliary market for movies. A few such issues are briefly introduced here.

### Adaptation: *How Different Are DVDs from Movies? From VHS Tapes?*

As compared to the differences between video tapes and movies, it is hypothesized that DVDs are much less similar to movies than video tapes are. It is undoubtedly true that for some people at some times, there is very little to differentiate renting a video tape from renting a DVD (although the visual and audio quality of the DVD may be higher). Nevertheless, many DVDs are designed to be products that differ from the movie and that are marketed to be sold to consumers. With added features and random access to DVD chapters plus marketing programs designed to sell (through distribution, pricing, and communication) the DVD, it would be surprising if consumers did not regard DVDs as differing from video tapes.

There are many issues to be raised. Here is a sampling. To what extent are different forecasting approaches required, and to what extent will the various movie and video products act as complements and substitutes for each other? How should the DVD product be designed? Should there be a product line of DVD products for each title? How should they be released over time? Traditionally, Hollywood studios have distributed their products through theaters and video retailers where the movie is the critical product. However, as DVDs become just another product sold by mass merchandisers and multi-line retailers, how will distribution channel arrangements change? If DVD sales become the dominant revenue stream, should Hollywood studios optimize their marketing for the DVD market (e.g., release that romantic comedy DVD for Valentine's Day and then determine the movie release date, attempt to engage the stars in intensive publicity campaigns around when a DVD is released?).

## Price Discrimination

To the frustration of economists and marketers, but not necessarily Hollywood executives, "in any given movie theater, all movies are priced the same regardless of their success and potential and regardless of the general demand conditions" (Orbach and Einav, 2001, abstract).[12] This lack of price discrimination has deep roots in the industry and may reflect important strategic considerations.

Video retailers have practiced some limited forms of price discrimination, largely on the basis of time – new movies typically rent for a higher price or shorter time period than do older ones. Although the DVD market is still in its early stages, there appears to be far more price dispersion, and future research questions surround the pricing strategies for DVDs. Will the combination of product-line differentiation among DVDs of the same title and DVDs based on movies, television shows, and live performances accelerate this process? An important issue in price-discrimination strategies is whether consumers perceive it as fair.

---

[12] It should be noted that the wholesale price at which studios rent their movies to theaters varies considerably by appeal of the movie and time since release. Also, and by contrast, outside North America, ticket prices sometimes vary by movie. For example, in December 2003 in Shanghai, the ticket prices for North American movies were observed by the author to be at least double that for locally produced films.

Recent attempts, as exemplified by Amazon.com's effort to charge different prices to new and established customers, suggest that consumers will accept some but not all approaches to price discrimination as being fair. Moreover, as DVDs are sold through mass merchants with different objectives, the ability of Hollywood studios to anticipate the retail pricing will likely be diminished. Further, if DVD prices continue to decline (according to MPAA from an average of $25.31 in 1998 to $20.78 in 2002), the DVD if nothing else could become a competitor to CDs, at least for the original sound track of movies![13] In summary, there appear to be a number of intriguing research questions to be studied in the area of product-line pricing.

### *Piracy*

This chapter started by noting that in the movie industry, time is of the essence. Piracy makes it more so, with pirated copies of movies appearing at various quality levels soon after a movie's (or a DVD's) release. In the timing-game section of this chapter, I examined how the introduction of a video can drive theater attendance to zero. Adding the effect of piracy to the timing-game model would seem to be quite interesting. Because not all consumers are willing to purchase or view pirated copies of movies, or have access to them, an interesting model could be built based on assessing the impact on revenues for different forms of piracy. Other interesting questions are: How much should be invested in technology to prevent piracy?, and How inconvenient is that technology to consumers? At what stage is the cost of deterring piracy offset by the disutility to consumers of dealing with piracy-protection procedures? Alternatively, could consumers be convinced that it is unfair to enjoy pirated versions of movies? With models of fairness and equity being reported in the

---

[13] For example, on April 4, 2003, the CD for the soundtrack of *8 Mile* was advertised on Amazon.com at $13.49 (or $15.99 for the version with explicit lyrics) and the DVD at $17.99 (or $20.23 for the edition with censored bonus features).

consumer-behavior literature, interesting research questions can be raised in this domain as well.

## CONCLUSION

Videos, foreign box office, television, consumer products, and myriad other tangible and intangible products are linked to the movies. In total, these ancillary products account for more revenue than the movie itself. Does this mean that the movie should follow the other markets or that the movie should lead the other markets? Such a question defies a simple answer.

This chapter highlighted a number of research questions about the ancillary products but focused on the video (tape and DVD) rental and sales industry, as this is the major source of income. Hopefully, these questions will stimulate interest in further research into the ever-entertaining entertainment industry.

### REFERENCES

Elberse, Anita, and Jehoshua Eliashberg. 2003. "Demand and Supply Dynamics for Sequentially Released Products in International Markets: The Case of Motion Pictures," *Marketing Science*, 22(3): 329–54.

Eliashberg, Jehoshua, Jedid-Jah Jonker, Mohanbir S. Sawhney, and Berend Wierenga. 2000. "MOVIEMOD: An Implementable Decision Support System for Pre-release Market Evaluation of Motion Pictures," *Marketing Science*, 19(3): 226–43.

Groves, Don. 2003. "Major Overseas Revenue Grows 18%," *Variety*, April 8.

Hawkins, Robert J. 1995. "*Lion King*: An Industry in Itself," *The San Diego Union Tribune*, March 2.

Jedidi, Kamel, Robert E. Krider, and Charles B. Weinberg. 1998. "Clustering at the Movies," *Marketing Letters*, 9(4): 393–405.

Krider, Robert E., and Charles B. Weinberg. 1998. "Competitive Dynamics and the Introduction of New Products: The Motion Picture Timing Game," *Journal of Marketing Research*, 35(1): 1–15.

Lehmann, Donald R., and Charles B. Weinberg. 2000. "Sales via Sequential Distribution Channels: An Application to Movie Audiences," *Journal of Marketing*, 64(3): 13–33.

Mortimer, Julie H. 2004. "Vertical Contracts in the Video Rental Industry," unpublished manuscript, Economics Department, Harvard University.

Orbach, B. Y., and Liran Einav. 2001. "Uniform Prices for Differentiated Goods: The Case of the Movie-Theater Industry," *Harvard Olin Discussion Paper* No. 337.

Prasad, Ashutosh, Bart Bronnenberg, and Vijay Mahajan. 2004. "Product Entry Timing in Dual Distribution Channels: The Case of the Movie Industry," *Review of Marketing Science*, 2(1), Article 4.

Ravid, S. Abraham, and Suman Basuroy. 2004. "Beyond Morality and Ethics: Executive Objective Function, the R-Rating Puzzle and the Production of Violent Movies," *Journal of Business*, 77(2).

Reavis, Cate. 1998. "Disney's *The Lion King* (A): The $2 Billion Movie," Harvard Business School, Case 9–899–041, October 14.

Swami, Sanjeev, Martin L. Puterman, and Charles B. Weinberg. 2001. "Play It Again, Sam? Optimal Replacement Policies for a Motion Picture Exhibitor," *Manufacturing and Service Operations Management*, 3(3): 369–86.

Waterman, David, and Sung-Choon Lee. 2002a. "Theatrical Feature Film Trade and Media Policies in the United States, Europe, and Japan since the 1950s," unpublished manuscript, Indiana University.

Waterman, David, and Sung-Choon Lee. 2002b. "Time Consistency and the Distribution of Theatrical Films: An Empirical Study of the Video Window," unpublished manuscript, Indiana University.

# Appendix

Consider the following sequential distribution problem: A studio must determine the optimal time to introduce a specific title to the video market. Further, assume that there are only two distribution channels and that industry practice determines which is the prior channel (e.g., theatrical release before video release).

## GENERAL STRUCTURE

Let $\Pi_1^B(t)$ be the profit rate at time $t$ from the first channel (e.g., movie theaters) before the second channel (e.g., video) is opened, and let $\Pi_1^A(t)$ be profit rate at time $t$ from the first channel after the second channel is opened at time $t_2$. (Setting $\Pi_1^A(t) = 0$ for $t \geq t_2$ allows for the case where opening the second channel completely eliminates sales and, consequently, profit in the first channel.) Let $\Pi_2(t, t_2)$ for $t \geq t_2$ be the profit rate from the second channel. Using a continuous model and assuming a discount rate $\rho$, the distributor attempts to maximize cumulative profit by choosing the optimal time $(t_2^*)$ to open the second channel.

# Appendix

$$P(t_2) = \int_0^{t_2} \Pi_1^B(t) \exp(-\rho t)\, dt + \int_{t_2}^{\infty} \Pi_1^A(t) \exp(-\rho t)\, dt$$

$$+ \int_{t_2}^{\infty} \Pi_2(t,\, t_2) \exp(-\rho t)\, dt \tag{1}$$

A further generalization of this structure involves incorporating other decision variables explicitly in the profit objective. Advertising strategies and prices are two examples.

Maximization of (1) with respect to $t_2$ yields an implicit expression of the optimal time to open the second channel. Next, the analysis is customized for the movie industry.

## MOVIE AND VIDEO DEMAND

Consistent with Krider and Weinberg (1998), Lehmann and Weinberg model a movie's revenue in the first channel as an exponential function:

$$M^B(t) = m_1^B \exp(-m_2 t) \qquad \text{for } 0 \leq t < t_2 \tag{2A}$$

$$M^A(t) = m_1^A \exp(-m_2 t) \qquad \text{for } t \geq t_2 \tag{2B}$$

$$\text{where } m_1^B > m_1^A \geq 0 \text{ and } m_2 > 0$$

In other words, a movie opens with a box-office sales rate of $m_1^B$ (at $t = 0$) and then declines at a rate of $m_2$. The effect of releasing a video is to decrease the market potential for the movie so that $0 \leq m_1^A < m_1^B$, but Lehmann and Weinberg assume the decay in revenue persists at the same rate, $m_2$.[1] In practice, theater sales generally drop to approximately zero when a movie is released to video. For the movies studied in Lehmann and Weinberg, box-office revenues when the video was released never

---

[1] The first channel's sales rate is assumed to drop from $M^B(t_2)$ to $M^A(t_2)$ exactly when sales in the second channel begin. Other formulations could be developed that allow for sales to drop earlier, in anticipation of the second channel being opened, or later, allowing for a delay in the second channel's effect. The immediate decay appears to be most appropriate, given the wide availability of video stores.

exceeded 3 percent of first-week's revenue. Therefore, Lehmann and Weinberg set $M^A(t) = m_1^A = 0$.

Video-rental demand is also assumed (and shown empirically in Lehmann and Weinberg) to follow a similar exponential decline, so that $V(t, t_2)$ represents the video-rental rate at time $t$ for a video released at $t_2$.

$$V(t, t_2) = v_1(t_2) \exp\left(-v_2^A(t - t_2)\right) \qquad \text{for } t \geq t_2 \qquad (3)$$

The video opens with rentals of $v_1(t_2)$, where $\dfrac{dv_1}{dt_2} < 0$. In other words, the longer the video release is delayed, the lower the potential video rentals. To reflect this compactly,

$$v_1(t_2) = v_1 \exp\left(-v_2^B t_2\right) \qquad (4)$$

where $v_1$ is the (implicit) rental potential of the video if it had been released simultaneously with the movie.

### RETAILER'S OPTIMAL ORDER QUANTITY

$V(u)$ = rental-demand rate per video store at time $u = (t - t_2)$ after the video's release

$\quad = v_1 \exp(-v_2^B t_2) \exp(-v_2^A u)$

$p$ = price to retailer per video

$r$ = rental fee per copy (assumed to be constant)

$n$ = number of rental turns per copy by the time period; for example, 3 per week

$h$ = holding cost per period per unit

$\ell$ = out-of-stock lost sales cost per period

$q$ = number of video tapes ordered

$\tau$ = time after video's release at which video-rental demand equals rental capacity of the store

$T$ = time horizon for which videos are held, at the end of which they have no salvage value

# Appendix

The time $\tau$ after the video's release when demand $[V(\tau)]$ equals the rental capacity, $nq$, can be found by solving the following equation for $\tau$:

$$nq = V(\tau) = v_1 \exp\left(-v_2^B t_2\right) \exp\left(-v_2^A \tau\right)$$
$$= k_1 \exp\left(-v_2^A \tau\right)$$
$$\text{where } k_1 = v_1 \exp\left(-v_2^B t_2\right)$$

This yields

$$\tau = \left(\frac{1}{v_2^A}\right) \ln\left(\frac{k_1}{nq}\right)$$

The video retailer's cumulative profits from ordering $q$ copies of a video (when the video is released) are defined as follows:

$$P_R = r\left[\int_0^\tau nq\, du + \int_\tau^T k_1 \exp\left(-v_2^A u\right) du\right]$$
$$- pq - hqT - \ell \int_0^\tau \left(k_1 \exp\left(-v_2^A u\right) - nq\right) du \qquad (5)$$

Notice that this formulation assumes unsatisfied demand due to capacity constraints leads to lost sales.

Simplifying from Lehmann and Weinberg to concentrate on the critical issues, assume that there is neither holding cost ($h = 0$) nor lost sales cost ($\ell = 0$) beyond that of the lost sales revenue, so that the optimal solution (i.e., order quantity) to (5) becomes

$$q^* = \frac{k_1}{n} \exp\left(-\left(\frac{p}{rn}\right) v_2^A\right) = \frac{v_1}{n} \exp\left(-v_2^B t_2\right) \exp\left(-\left(\frac{pv_2^A}{rn}\right)\right)$$

## MANUFACTURER'S (FILM DISTRIBUTOR'S) OPTIMAL RELEASE TIME TO THE RETAILER

Assume that each sale achieves a constant gross margin for the distributor of $M_T$ in the first (theater) channel and $M_V$ in the second video channel.

# Appendix

$M_V$ depends on the price at which the movie distributor sells videos to the retailer and the number ($N$) of video stores.

Combining these equations and recalling that $m_1^A = 0$, the cumulative profit for the movie distributor is

$$P(t_2) = \int_0^{t_2} M_T m_1^B e^{-m_2^t} e^{-\rho t}\, dt + M_V q^*(t_2, p) e^{-\rho t_2}$$

or

$$P(t_2) = \int_0^{t_2} M_T m_1^B \exp(-m_2 t) \exp(-\rho t)\, dt + M_V q^*(t_2, p) \exp(-\rho t_2) \tag{6}$$

Setting the discount rate $\rho = 0$ for expositional convenience (because it has minimal impact on the results), the cumulative profit function can be rewritten as

$$P(t_2) = \left( M_T \frac{m_1^B}{m_2} \right) (1 - \exp(-m_2 t_2))$$
$$+ M_V \frac{v_1}{n} \exp\left(-v_2^B t_2\right) \exp\left(-\frac{p v_2^A}{rn}\right) \tag{7}$$
$$= \left( \begin{array}{c} \text{Profit from} \\ \text{theater market} \end{array} \right) + \left( \begin{array}{c} \text{Profit from} \\ \text{video market} \end{array} \right)$$

Solving yields the optimal time to release as

$$t_2^* = \frac{1}{\left(m_2 - v_2^B\right)} \left\{ \ln\left[ \frac{m_1^B n M_T}{v_2^B v_1 M_V} \right] + \left( \frac{p}{r} \frac{v_2^A}{n} \right) \right\} \tag{8}$$

# Index

# Index

# Index

# Index

# Index

# Index

# Index

# Index

# Index

213

# Index